HEART OF A
HOOSIER

HEART OF A

A YEAR OF INSPIRATION FROM IU MEN'S BASKETBALL

HOOSIER

DEL DUDUIT *and* **MICHELLE MEDLOCK ADAMS**

AN IMPRINT OF
INDIANA UNIVERSITY PRESS

This book is a publication of

Quarry Books
an imprint of

Indiana University Press
Office of Scholarly Publishing
Herman B Wells Library 350
1320 East 10th Street
Bloomington, Indiana 47405 USA

iupress.org

© 2021 by Del Duduit and Michelle Medlock Adams

Manufactured in the United States of America
First printing 2021

Cataloging information is available from the
Library of Congress.
ISBN 978-0-253-05696-2 (hardback)
ISBN 978-0-253-05697-9 (paperback)
ISBN 978-0-253-05698-6 (ebook)

From Del . . .

To my late parents, Buddy and Barb Duduit,
who took time to show me right from wrong and
always supported me.

From Michelle . . .

In honor of my late parents, Walter and Marion Medlock,
who raised me to love God, my family, and
the Indiana Hoosiers.
I am forever grateful.
This one's for you, Mom and Dad.

CONTENTS

IU PLAYERS

IU COACHES

HEART OF A
HOOSIER

INTRODUCTION

Michelle Medlock Adams

I WENT TO MY FIRST IU basketball game when I was six years old, and that was it. I never wanted to miss another one. Even as a child, as I stood and belted out, "Go IU, fight, fight, fight!" I knew I was part of something very special.

I was right.

Being an IU fan—being part of the Hoosier Nation—has been one of the great loves of my life. It's a legacy of love that my parents passed down to me, and it's one that I've passed down to my children. I'm guessing you share that same love for the Hoosiers, or you wouldn't have picked up this book.

Our hope is that you'll relive some of your favorite IU Basketball memories and find inspiration in those stories as well as learn some Hoosier basketball history you might not have known. But more than anything, we hope each entry challenges you to be better, dream bigger, and never give up. If there were ever a time in history when we needed a little more encouragement and a lot more understanding, it's now. We pray you'll find those things in the pages of this book too.

We want you to know that as we wrote this book, we pictured you sitting across the table from us, drinking a Coke and eating a Hinkle's hamburger. We already consider you our friend. And if you're a die-hard Hoosiers fan, well then that makes you family. Thanks for taking this journey with us. And, last but not least . . . say it loud and proud: we are IU! (You're doing the arm motions right now, aren't you? Love it!)

IU TRADITIONS

WEEK 1 | WHAT'S YOUR MOTIVATION?

Del Duduit

WILLIAM TELL OVERTURE

When the third television time-out is called in the second half at a home Indiana University basketball game, pandemonium breaks loose. The IU pep band performs the "William Tell Overture," getting the crowd pumped up while the cheerleaders race around the court displaying eighteen Hoosier flags. The fans love it.

The tradition began during the 1979 season and has been described as the greatest time-out in college basketball. If the Hoosiers are winning, it inspires the team and crowd to keep going. If Indiana is behind in the game, the band and cheerleaders motivate the fans and squad to fight back.

The overture to the opera *William Tell* was the theme song for the Lone Ranger and his mighty "high ho Silver, away." Classic cartoons such as Bugs Bunny and *The Flintstones* also used the music in many scenes. The song was also featured in many motion pictures such as *The Princess Diaries* and *A Clockwork Orange*.

The original score, composed by Gioachino Rossini, premiered at the Paris Opéra in 1829. It lasts about twelve minutes and describes a picture of life in the Swiss Alps. It's a symphony broken down into four parts:

Prelude: Dawn—this signifies the calm before a storm
Storm—the event you run and seek shelter from

Ranz des vaches—daybreak or a calming when the storm begins to pass
Finale: March of the Swiss Soldiers—a victory and daylight

What inspires you to finish the game? Do you need a little boost to bolster your spirits and encourage you to keep going?

BREAK THE PRESS

Are you losing the game in the second half? Do you need someone or something to encourage you to continue? Maybe you're ahead in life and don't want to lose focus on why you're playing hard to win. Or perhaps you're about to face a major storm in your life. Your doctor may have delivered some tough news. Maybe the person you were dating has ended the relationship. In times like these, it can be difficult to see a positive outcome. But if you keep moving forward, the storm will pass and break up, and you will once again see the light of day. You might also make a comeback and stand victorious in the middle of the court.

SLAM DUNK

We all face trials and problems. It's part of life. Difficulties can either make you weak and frightened or stir up the spirit in you to keep fighting to win the game. The first thing you must do to overcome the storm is be prepared for it to hit. A good basketball coach will have his team ready to withstand runs by the opposition. When the storm clouds form and head your way, stand up and face the issues. Don't run from them, but instead meet them head-on.

Lean on friends and family to help see you through the rough times. Sometimes you need to vent, but refrain from taking out your problems on others. Be determined to withstand the circumstances and learn from the moment. This may help you later assist someone else who might face a similar situation. Maintain a positive attitude, and be ready to get back on the court when the storm has passed. Anticipate the time-out, and raise your flags to run around the gym in victory.

How can you withstand the storms of life?

_____

_____

_____

_____

_____

_____

_____

_____

_____

_____

_____

_____

_____

_____

_____

_____

_____

_____

_____

_____

_____

_____

_____

_____

_____

_____

_____

_____

_____

_____

_____

_____

_____

WEEK 2 | GIVE HONOR WHERE HONOR IS DUE

Michelle Medlock Adams

SENIOR SPEECHES—DAMON BAILEY DOES IT RIGHT

Just the mention of Senior Night speeches brings smiles to the faces of diehard IU Basketball fans. Those speeches are as stirring and beloved as the team's candy-striped warm-up pants and the playing of the *William Tell* "Overture" during the iconic second-half time-out.

It's tradition.

Coach Bob Knight began the custom back in 1973, and it continues to this day. After the last home game of the season, all senior players have the opportunity to address the coaches, their fellow players, their families, and, of course, the faithful fans. Some give long, eloquent speeches while others make it short and sweet. Jarrad Odle, a 2002 senior and the scrappy forward from Swayzee, Indiana, whom so many fans had grown to appreciate, might've said it best: "I put four years in for you guys. You can give me twenty minutes."[1]

It's often an emotional night filled with tears, laughter, and lots of nostalgia. While I have had many favorite senior speeches over the years, Damon Bailey's sweet words to his younger sister, Courtney, who had been battling leukemia, warm my heart the most. (Full disclosure: I was born and raised in Lawrence County, Indiana, and was a varsity cheerleader when Damon played at Bedford North Lawrence High School. So, I might be a bit biased . . . but I don't care. Damon's words brought everyone to tears.) When Damon took his turn at the mic, he shared,

"I get cheered. I get all the hoopla because I can dribble a basketball and shoot a basketball, but Courtney is the one who should be cheered. She's been through a lot more than I have."

Here was one of the most popular athletes to ever come out of Indiana. He was recruited as an eighth grader by Coach Bob Knight and went on to become Indiana's all-time high school leading scorer—a record that still stands. He'd earned numerous awards in his high school and college careers, yet he didn't revisit any of those accolades in his speech. Instead, when he got the opportunity to speak in front of a captive audience of adoring fans, he humbly honored his sister for her courage to fight and beat leukemia.

That stood out to me. It was a classy move, but that's not why Damon spoke those words. He wasn't coached by a media guru on what to say or how best to say it. He simply spoke from the heart, honoring family above all of the hoopla surrounding his storied career. And isn't that what life is all about? When the spotlight is no longer shining on you, when reporters no longer clamor for your remarks, when fans no longer chant your name or even remember it, who is left? Your family. Your friends who are like family. Those who know you best and still love you when you aren't at your best.

You may not have a special Senior Night to honor those you love, but you can send them a card or simply give them a call, letting them know how very much they mean to you.

BREAK THE PRESS

Do you have trouble putting your feelings into words? How long has it been since you told the people you hold most dear just how much you love and appreciate them? It's not too late. But don't let another day pass without saying what is on your heart. If someone inspired you or helped you achieve a goal, recognize that person's contribution to your life. You never know how badly that person may need to hear those words.

SLAM DUNK

Life is busy. Days turn into weeks and weeks into years and years into decades in what seems like a blink of an eye. So seize the moment! Make it a priority to bless those who have inspired, encouraged, helped, taught, coached, and blessed you. From a simple "I'm just calling to say thank you" to writing a heartfelt letter to posting a public tribute—tell them.

How can you best honor the people who have inspired you or left an imprint on your heart?

_____

_____

_____

_____

_____

_____

_____

_____

_____

_____

_____

_____

_____

_____

_____

_____

_____

_____

_____

_____

_____

_____

_____

_____

_____

NOTE

1. Matt Dollinger, "Senior Night Is Players' Final Chance to Bid Farewell," *Indiana Daily Student*, March 3, 2009, https://www.idsnews.com/article/2009/03/senior-night-is-players-final-chance-to-bid-farewell.

WEEK 3 | CANDY-STRIPED LEGACY

Michelle Medlock Adams

BEFORE EACH AND EVERY INDIANA basketball game, you'll see the Hoosiers take the court wearing their signature candy-striped warm up pants. It's a tradition that's stuck around for half a century—but have you ever stopped to ask yourself, "Where did those bold red-and-white pants come from?"

You might be surprised to learn that it was actually Coach Bob Knight's idea! Knight's 1971–72 team were the first to don the iconic warm-up attire as well as the first team to play in Assembly Hall. As wild as those pants are, they really weren't too outlandish for the '70s. In fact, they were right on trend . . . but more for performers or rock musicians.

So why were they chosen for Indiana's warm-ups?

"I just liked them," Coach Knight told Bob Hammel, his coauthor of *The Power of Negative Thinking.* "They were different."[1]

Soon, Indiana became known for its loud, colorful pants. They were an icon of the team and of the university. Fashion trends have come and gone, but the Hoosiers have kept their candy-striped pants. Although the IU warm-ups may not be as trendy as other teams' choices, the legacy of Indiana Basketball will never go out of style. The IU court is the only place you'll find these pants—aside from on the legs of IU fans around the country. When you see the candy-striped warm-ups, you immediately know you're in the company of Hoosiers.

What kind of mark will you leave in your work, your home, and your life? What will remind people of you when they see it? What are you known for?

BREAK THE PRESS

Entrepreneur, author, and speaker Gary Vaynerchuk has said, "Please think about your legacy, because you're writing it every day." The truth is, each and every day is a building block in the legacy you are leaving. The choices you make leave a lasting impact on the people and the world around you, even when you're not thinking about it. When you dare to do something new and bold, you have the opportunity to create something that will last long after your own involvement. And the earlier you start, the more results you will see come from your actions.

SLAM DUNK

Why did Coach Knight choose the candy-striped pants? He said, "I just liked them." Creating your legacy doesn't need to be complex. Look at the things you like, the things you want to see in the world, and the things you have the power to do. You don't have to be influential or charismatic; just live your life unafraid to do things. Whatever you do, it will leave some mark on the world. Dare to do something new and create a legacy.

What would you like people to think of when they think of you? What can you do today to intentionally work toward creating the legacy you desire?

_____

_____

_____

_____

_____

_____

_____

NOTE

1. Chris Mahr, "How Indiana Began Wearing Its Trademark Candy-striped Warmup Pants," Yahoo! Sports, March 8, 2013, https://sports.yahoo.com/blogs/ncaab-the-dagger/indiana-began-wearing-trademark-candy-striped-warmup-pants-161242553--ncaab.html.

WEEK 4 | THE SIMPLE THING IN LIFE

Del Duduit

SPORTS UNIFORMS AND JERSEYS CAN display a wide range of attractive traits. Many schools and universities have gone to great lengths to make bold statements when their teams run onto the field of play.

The University of Oregon has taken the art of the uniform to a whole new level.

In 2006, the football team had 384 different combinations they could have worn in the thirteen games they played. The Ducks featured jerseys, helmets, socks, and shoes in a wide variety of school colors. When the team debuted a new look in the 2006 Las Vegas Bowl, the metallic yellow helmets with silver flames boosted the possible combinations to 512.

Keep in mind, there were just over a dozen games scheduled for the season. But the crew responsible for coordinating the uniform schedule must have been exhausted by the end of each week. Imagine trying to track all the different combinations and making sure each player had the exact same uniform. This took considerable planning and attention to detail. But the players looked amazing when they ran onto the field.

In contrast, the Indiana Hoosiers basketball team has had one basic look for years, and it works. And this is the way the fans like it—they embrace tradition and don't like to bring attention to what the players wear. Instead, the team focuses on winning.

The IU team is widely known for its simple game jerseys. The uniform features the team colors—cream and crimson—with the name of the school across the front of the chest, and the numbers appear right below and on the back. Nothing more and nothing less.

Most team jerseys are personalized, with the player's name on the back. Not Indiana's. The nameless tops promote teamwork and unity. No one player is more important than the team.

For this reason, the Hoosiers have never retired any numbers. There are no jerseys in frames hanging from the rafters to celebrate phenomenal players, as you see in many arenas. The only banners that hang in Assembly Hall are NCAA Championship flags captured by the team.

BREAK THE PRESS

Have you ever been recognized for a major accomplishment? Did this make you feel special? Of course it did. Do you like to receive an award with your name on it? Do you like attention, and do you enjoy having your name out there for everyone to see? We see names on the backs of most jerseys in athletics. We also see the names of stars in television and movie credits, and a byline tells us who authored a story or article. Is identity a good thing?

SLAM DUNK

Receiving recognition is a great, but it can also shift your focus away from your team if you're not careful. If you have a team of professionals at work and one is recognized more than others, it can lead to jealousy. If you make a mistake and the entire world knows about it, then embarrassment may follow.

There is nothing wrong with having a simple and productive lifestyle, just like the Hoosiers. They have produced five national championships and eight Final Four appearances. No one person is responsible for these accomplishments.

Instead of bringing attention to yourself, consider ways for your team or family to be praised. You can accomplish this by limiting criticism of others and lowering expectations. Make a point to be present at your kids' events. Put in the effort to be nice and considerate to others. Prioritize family time, and reduce your workload if it interferes with the things in life that really matter. Don't be afraid to fail, and make sure you laugh a lot, especially at yourself.

You don't have to be flamboyant to be remembered. Just consistently produce.

How can you make your life simple?

_____
_____
_____
_____
_____
_____
_____
_____
_____
_____
_____
_____
_____
_____
_____
_____
_____
_____
_____
_____
_____
_____
_____
_____
_____
_____
_____
_____
_____

WEEK 5 | BLEEDING CREAM AND CRIMSON

Michelle Medlock Adams

GROWING UP A PROUD INDIANA University fan, I had no idea that not everyone shared my love for the Hoosiers and Coach Bob Knight. It wasn't until I was in junior high and found myself getting into the occasional verbal confrontation with those who didn't share my fondness for the Hoosiers and The General that I realized not all Indiana residents backed IU. Some, I discovered, cheered for Purdue and even Kentucky! I just couldn't understand it.

My parents had season tickets in section E, so I grew up going to most every home men's basketball game. Even as a very young girl, I knew the camaraderie and passion I shared with the thousands of fans standing and singing the Indiana fight song was very special. (You're singing along right now in your head, aren't you?)

I had always looked forward to studying journalism at IU's Bloomington campus, but my parents had other plans. They made a deal with me—they would pay for my college education if I would go to a small Christian university for my freshman year, and then if I still wanted to attend IU, they would let me transfer to IU Bloomington's campus to finish my education. Though I hated missing my freshman year at IU, I agreed and made my way to Asbury College, about thirty minutes outside of Lexington, Kentucky. Of course, you know what's in Lexington— lots and lots of diehard University of Kentucky fans. I'll never forget driving into Lexington to get dorm necessities and realizing I wasn't in friendly territory. Back then, I drove a little red Fiero that proudly displayed an "IU Fan" bumper sticker. I heard lots of honks, and they weren't welcoming. You know how I know? Because they were often accompanied by the flying of the bird and the occasional "IU sucks!" Yes, those UK fans were just as passionate as the Hoosier Nation, and I was definitely outnumbered. No matter. I still wore my IU spiritwear and cheered on my beloved Hoosiers until I could transfer and once again be around others who bled cream and crimson.

Since graduating from IU in 1991, my travels have taken me all across this great land, and you know what I've discovered? There are a lot of us. IU fans are everywhere, and we tend to find one another. At an amusement park in Florida, I noticed someone sporting an IU hat and struck up a conversation about news of future recruits. As a speaker at a writers' conference, the last line of my bio read, "When not writing or teaching writing, Michelle enjoys cheering on IU sports teams and all things leopard print"—which caused several attendees to seek me out and share, "I bleed cream and crimson, too!" We are drawn to one another. You might say we're one big happy Hoosier family. We're loyal to a fault, and we're passionate about our players, our coaches, and our traditions. We'll defend our beloved Hoosiers to the end. We are IU fans, and we're proud of it.

BREAK THE PRESS

How long have you been an IU fan? If you're like me, your answer is "For as long as I can remember." You can't be fickle and be an IU fan. It's a commitment. They'll break your heart once in a while, but you'll come back for more because the love runs deep.

What else in your life brings you that kind of joy and heartbreak but is so worth it? Family? Your chosen profession? I hope you're passionate about things that matter, and I pray you live life to the fullest every single day. Because that's how we roll in the Hoosier Nation.

SLAM DUNK

Another loyal IU fan, John Cougar Mellencamp, once sang, "You've got to stand for something or you'll fall for anything." Standing up for a team you back. Defending something or someone you love. Those are admirable actions. Just be careful that your passionate backing or beliefs don't cross over into the obsessive realm. Be a diehard fan, but do it in a way that represents the integrity of Indiana Basketball. Show your Indiana pride, but be a fan IU can be proud of, too.

Besides Indiana Basketball, what else brings you joy? What else are you passionate about, would defend no matter what, or feel is worth your precious time? Jot a few of those things down. If your list is lacking, why not write down a few possible passions you'd like to pursue?

WEEK 6 | HAIL TO OLD IU!

Michelle Medlock Adams

WHEN THE IU FIGHT SONG plays, my heart beats a little faster. (I even had it as my ringtone for a while, and every time it rang, it made me happy.) The students, the alumni, the staff, the fans . . . no Hoosier can help but clap along or keep from cheering, "Go IU, fight, fight, fight!" Everyone also loves "Hail to Old IU," which has been the official IU alma mater for more than a century—it was performed for the first time in 1893 by the IU Glee Club. You'll hear both songs played several times at every home game because they get the fans all revved up!

Singing school songs is such a fun and powerful tradition. Music has a way of getting into your soul and setting it on fire. Music can motivate, soothe, and unite people. In fact, many researchers speculate that music existed before spoken language. American neuroscientist Daniel Levitin is quoted as saying, "Whenever humans come together for any reason, music is there: weddings, funerals, graduation from college, men marching off to war, stadium sporting events, a night on the town, prayer, a romantic dinner, mothers rocking their infants to sleep, and college students studying with music as a background."[1]

Music really does have a great impact on us as individuals and as groups. We can use music to invoke a certain feeling or desire. Pop songs from the '80s may cause people to feel energized. Smooth jazz may set off romantic vibes. Movie scores may inspire creativity. And the IU fight song? Well, it's designed to get people excited!

BREAK THE PRESS

Every good piece of music is written strategically. There is different music for different purposes. Music in movies is written to match the emotions of a particular scene in order to make viewers experience it more deeply. Think about it: how is the music different in a romance movie versus an action/thriller movie?

Some kinds of music can even change your behaviors. Video game music is written specifically to keep you focused and engaged, so it can actually be great background music for working or studying. Other music is meant to be calming, like Marconi Union's "Weightless"; it's so relaxing, people have recommended you don't listen to it while driving because it can make you drowsy.

SLAM DUNK

As you go about your everyday life, pay attention to the music you're hearing around you. What's playing over the grocery store speakers or on your car radio? How does the music in the TV show you're watching make you feel? Music is all around us, and when you pay attention to it, you can better understand and harness your emotions.

Take some time to put together playlists specifically for different times in your life. What music do you turn to when you work out? What about when you study? How about when you feel stressed? How can you change the music you hear to affect your emotions and actions? Maybe jot down some of your favorite songs and start compiling playlists to enhance your everyday life. (And don't forget to include the IU fight song on at least one of your lists.)

_____

_____

_____

_____

NOTE

1. Daniel J. Levitin, *This Is Your Brain on Music: The Science of a Human Obsession* (New York: Dutton, 2006), 6.

MONUMENTAL
MOMENTS

WEEK 7 | FOUL OUT YOUR FOES

Del Duduit

MARCH 4, 2012: INDIANA 85, PURDUE 74

Purdue came alive in the second half and made a serious run to win the game.

The Boilermakers got hot from the field and shot 51 percent while the Hoosiers struggled to connect on 35 percent of their attempts. The Indiana offense, which led by 15 points in the first half, was held at bay in the second stanza by the Purdue defense, which tended to foul down the stretch. But IU was effective from the line and held on to the lead from the charity stripe.

With about six minutes left in the game, Purdue pulled to within 7 points of the Hoosier lead. But solid performances from their top players led to the 85–74 win over Purdue in the Crimson & Gold Cup rivalry. The victory meant a season sweep of Purdue.

The Boilermakers' best player, Robbie Hummel, kept his team in the game with his three-point shooting performance. But he picked up his fifth foul with 1:12 to play in the game. Indiana's offense went at Hummel to make him commit the final foul and get him out of the game. They knew if they were able to sit down Purdue's best player, their odds of winning increased.

Indiana's Christian Watford poured in 19 points and had 16 rebounds while Cody Zeller chipped in with 13 points and 5 boards. But in the end, the Hoosiers held on for the win with grit and determination.

Have you ever been in a situation where you wanted to put distance between you and someone who disliked you? How do you handle moments where you have to be around a person who does not like you?

Does your boss or a coworker make you feel uneasy? Perhaps a family member snubs you in front of others. How do you respond?

BREAK THE PRESS

Put yourself in the following situation. You are a successful member of your sales team and work hard to see positive results. One of your teammates desires attention and wants to climb the ladder. They steal your ideas and take credit for your work. Or maybe they make fun of you in front of others for no reason. This can spark negative emotions. How do you handle it? Not everyone gets along in life. You will likely have to deal with people who have selfish and personal agendas.

SLAM DUNK

It takes a better person not to participate in the immature games some people play. This is difficult to do, and I become frustrated when I'm advised to be the bigger person in the heat of an emotional battle. Be the more mature person and turn the other cheek. This can be difficult to do at times, but it will make you stronger in the end. Live your life the best you can, with morals and convictions. Examine your own emotional needs and seek a solution instead of fueling the problem. Determine in your heart to be nice and kind and develop an attitude of forgiveness.

When you rise above the competition, you effectively foul out your opponent. Take the high road.

_____

_____

_____

_____

_____

_____

_____

WEEK 8 | PURSUE GREATNESS

Michelle Medlock Adams

1975–76 INDIANA HOOSIERS

A national championship stands as the goal of every team. Indiana's Coach Knight challenged his team to aim even higher.

The previous season had ended with a heartbreaking loss to Kentucky in the Elite Eight. The '75–'76 Hoosiers had championship dreams, but Coach Knight knew it was a team destined to make history. Bob Hammel, author and friend of Coach Knight, remembered the feeling heading into the '75–'76 season: "That's the one where [Knight] raised the sights to say, winning a championship won't be enough. If you guys play to your potential, you won't lose a game. Anything short of that is a disappointment. That's paraphrased, obviously, but that was the feeling."[1]

A loaded lineup featured future NBA number-two overall pick Scott May, who had earned accolades such as All-American, Big Ten Player of the Year, and National Player of the Year. May was joined by Quinn Buckner, Kent Benson, and Bob Wilkerson, who were all taken in the first round of the NBA draft as well.

Throughout the season, Indiana focused on perfection. Opening the season against defending champion UCLA, the Hoosiers started their quest by knocking off the Bruins. Throughout the season, there were close games and struggles, but with each obstacle, the Hoosiers rose to the challenge. It was one W after another.

Knight pushed the team. Intense practices prepared each player to succeed on game day. As Bobby Wilkerson shared, "I'll tell you part of the reason we were so good: under Coach Knight, the games seemed like a vacation."[2]

The tournament draw presented a difficult path to the championship. Facing Marquette in the Elite Eight, the number-two overall team in the nation, led to a change in the NCAA tournament. After the matchup, the committee decided to seed the tournament. Additionally, the Hoosiers encountered UCLA again, and when they reached the national championship game, they squared off against Michigan for the third time.

No team has since accomplished what the 1975–76 Hoosiers did—a perfect season and a national championship. Coach Knight had convinced them to dream bigger, give more, be better, and achieve the ultimate, and that's exactly what they did.

Where are the areas in your life where you have settled for less?

BREAK THE PRESS

Life presents opportunities to excel or to settle. Which one do you choose? Situations lure us to settle. A career sucks the life out of you, but you stay because at least you know what to expect. Friendships and dating relationships eat away at your sanity and your self-worth, yet you keep them going because, you tell yourself, "It could be worse." Settling for financial troubles seems to be easier than digging in and making changes. Rather than chase your dream, you watch others achieve theirs.

Settling is easy. Such a decision requires no effort on your part, other than doing what has been done before. But what if you could achieve something better? What if you could reach historic heights in your own life?

SLAM DUNK

Set higher goals and give all you have to reach those heights. Your dreams are important. The drive to achieve them burns inside of you, and you can reach them if only you can silence the voices that tell you to settle for less. You have only this life to make an impact. Believe in yourself. Push yourself. Find those who see potential in you and be accountable to them to set the bar higher. Achieving greatness will be worth the sacrifice. Those who settle look back with regret. Those who achieve greatness look back with satisfaction. Let's fall into the latter group.

What form of greatness can you begin working toward today?

_____

_____

_____

_____

_____

_____

_____

_____

_____

_____

_____

_____

_____

_____

_____

_____

_____

_____

_____

_____

_____

_____

NOTES

1. Zach Osterman, "1976 Indiana Hoosiers' Undefeated Season: An Oral History," *Indianapolis Star*, January 2, 2016, https://www.indystar.com/story/sports/college/indiana/2016/01/02/1976-indiana-hoosiers-undefeated-season-oral-history/78181576/.

2. Jack McCallum, "The Spirit of '76," *Vault*, March 19, 2001, https://vault.si.com/vault/2001/03/19/the-spirit-of-76-a-quarter-century-has-passed-since-there-has-been-a-champ ionthe-7576-indiana-hoosierstough-enough-to-go-undefeated.

WEEK 9 | JUST IN TIME

Del Duduit

DECEMBER 26, 2017: INDIANA 80, NOTRE DAME 77

The Hoosiers were off to a slow start.

They had just come off a loss to Indiana State and were 5-5 early in the season. Although the college basketball season is brief, it can seem long if a team has an undesirable start.

The Fighting Irish rolled into Indianapolis ranked eighteenth in the country and primed to take the title at the Crossroads Classic, an annual doubleheader tournament between the state's four highest-profile teams. But Juwan Morgan had other plans. He scored 19 of his career-high 34 points in the final eight minutes to boost the Hoosiers to an 80–77 win in overtime over Notre Dame. For Coach Archie Miller, it was a big win given his young stint at the helm.

Juwan poured in all of Indiana's points during an 8–0 run to force the extra period. He then was fouled with eleven seconds to play and went to the line. He missed, but IU grabbed the rebound and got the ball back to Juwan, who power-dunked the ball into the rim for the 87–77 lead with about eight seconds to play.

The junior All-Big Ten player dominated the game. He connected on thirteen of seventeen shots and pulled down eleven rebounds. He came through when Indiana needed him the most and propelled the Hoosiers to a big win at the right time. The tone was set early in the game, and Juwan delivered in a big way to defeat a top-twenty team.

Have you had to come through at the last minute? How did you perform?

BREAK THE PRESS

We sometime face tough choices in life and must decide what is most important. Maybe your boss wants you to spend more time at the office to prepare a presentation that could have valuable rewards for your company and your future. You have spent hours putting in overtime and leaving home early. Your wife understands and supports you; however, your children are a little confused. They want you to come home to play with them and help them with homework. Your wife could also use a break. Finally, the time comes when one of your kids has an important school function and asks you to attend. What will you do? It's equivalent to facing the number-ten ranked team in the country. Your family needs you to come through for them for the big win. Will you show up or stay at work?

SLAM DUNK

You should never have to choose between your family and work. We all must support our families financially, but there comes a time when it's overkill. Your family needs you more than your employer. A good company will encourage a good work-life balance. You may not face this exact scenario, but perhaps you have experienced a similar situation. Your family should come first as much as possible. This does not mean you will never have to work instead of attending a family function, but make sure it doesn't happen too often. Make sure you come through in the final moments for the big win and make your family the priority in your life.

Take advantage of downtime with your loved ones. During the weekend, put down your phone and focus on spending time and engaging in activities with your family. Above all, learn to say no to outside interferences. Everyone can get bogged down in life. Put yourself in a position where you can score all the team's points in the end and knock off a top-twenty team.

How can you come through when it counts?

_____

_____

_____

_____

_____

_____

_____

_____

_____

_____

_____

_____

_____

_____

_____

_____

_____

_____

_____

_____

_____

_____

_____

_____

_____

_____

_____

_____

WEEK 10 | LIVE LIKE A WINNER

Michelle Medlock Adams

TOUTED AS ONE OF THE greatest moments in March Madness history—and, of course, a fan favorite in IU Basketball—Keith Smart's sixteen-foot jumper in the final seconds of the 1987 national championship game against Syracuse still brings a big smile to my face.

My late father, Walter Medlock, had a recording of that game and a few other monumental IU matchups that were especially meaningful. (This was long before you could watch them on YouTube.) Sometimes, I'd hear that particular game playing in Dad's study, and I'd drop whatever I was doing and plop down in the chair next to him to watch sports history in the making . . . again. We had watched it together so many times I could almost recite word for word what announcers Brent Musburger and Billy Packer were going to say before they said it. But when we finally got to *the shot* and I heard the words "Indiana wins the championship! Keith Smart is the hero!" I celebrated all over again, every single time.

I actually enjoyed watching the game again and again, even when Syracuse ran up an eight-point lead in the second half. And when the Orangemen held Steve Alford scoreless those last four minutes of the game? I didn't even mind. Not once did I yell at the TV. You know why? Because I already knew the outcome of the game. I already knew Indiana won!

Wouldn't it be great if life were like that in real time? You know, living every day with joy in your heart, knowing that your story ended in victory so you could shrug off any obstacle or setback along the way.

Smiling through the stresses of life because you were guaranteed to win in the end. Yeah, that would be great. So, why not live like that anyway?

When you develop that kind of confidence and optimism, people will be drawn to you. They'll want to help you. Your positivity will literally attract success like a big ol' magnet. The same way your adversaries can smell fear, other winners can smell confidence. You're much more likely to become a winner if you already believe you are one. Charles Dickens once said, "The world belongs to those who set out to conquer it armed with self-confidence and good humor."

So, go ahead. Live like you already know the outcome of the game and you're Keith Smart with the winning, history-making shot.

BREAK THE PRESS

Do you ever struggle with self-doubt or fear? Those are very powerful emotions that can cripple you. But what if you didn't? What if you could go for your dreams with no hesitation and no fear? Wouldn't that be amazing? Just think of all you could accomplish if you knew that you would succeed in your endeavors. That's how we should approach our lives—cool, confident, and colossally happy.

SLAM DUNK

Fear of the "what ifs" can stop you from living life to its fullest. But don't let the unknown keep you from taking *the shot*. What if Keith Smart had been too afraid of missing the shot to take it? Of course, it wasn't luck that brought him to that moment when he automatically connected on the jumper and won the game. He was confident in his jump shot because he had practiced many hours under the tutelage of Coach Knight. Smart had been prepared for a scenario just like that, and when the situation presented itself, he stepped up and revealed the winner he had always been. It's time for you to do the same.

What fears are keeping you from reaching your full potential, and how can you overcome those fears?

_____

_____

_____

WEEK 11 | DON'T LET UP

Del Duduit

The Hoosiers had just knocked off the second-ranked Ohio State Buckeyes and were facing another Big Ten rival in Michigan. Sometimes a team can experience an emotional letdown when coming off a big win. This can be due to circumstances like exhaustion or mental fatigue. Other times, it can be from overconfidence. In any case, Indiana Coach Tom Crean was aware of this and had prepared his team to play the Michigan Wolverines.

Christian Watford had a complete game. The junior scored 25 points and hit one of two free throws with 2.9 seconds left in the game to boost Indiana to a 73–71 win over number-sixteen Michigan. The Hoosiers played tough and with grit and never once trailed during the game. But the Wolverines would not go down without a fight. With just over seven minutes to play, Michigan trailed by 10 points and put together a charge.

Indiana led 65–55 after Victor Oladipo slammed home a bucket, but Michigan responded. Trey Burke hit a three-pointer and then scored on a fast break to cut the Indiana lead to 68–65. Tim Hardaway grabbed a turnover and made the easy dunk to tie the game 68–68. But Indiana's Verdell Jones broke the tie with two free throws with 2:50 left, then hit a jumper with 23.9 seconds left, boosting the lead to 72–68.

The Wolverines found a three-pointer from Stu Douglass with 2.9 seconds left that made the score 72–71. Watford connected on a free throw, and Michigan's Zack Novak heaved the ball from half court in a desperate attempt to win, but the shot was off the mark.

To their credit, Michigan's players never backed down and had a chance to win in the end. And to the Hoosiers' credit, they did not allow the fact that they had beaten the number-two team in the nation a few days earlier affect how they played. They were in a battle and stayed strong.

How do you respond to pressure? Do you come out on top, or do you let the stress bring you down?

BREAK THE PRESS

Does pent-up frustration get to you? Perhaps you reach a boiling point and let off steam. Maybe you don't like to have deadlines thrust upon you at work. Or you might find yourself involved in a personal dispute you find uncomfortable. Does this sound familiar? This is life. It's a game of five on five every day. You win some big games and lose some close ones.

SLAM DUNK

The way you handle stress and the pressures of daily life is important. When you come off a big win, like Indiana's win against Ohio State, there is no room to let your guard down. You must stay on the path of personal and emotional success. One way to better equip yourself to handle unforeseen stresses in your daily routine is to participate in physical activity. Go to the gym and exercise—make time for yourself. Try not to stay up too late, and get plenty of sleep. Choose a friend you can talk to, and consider writing down your activities or thoughts in a diary. Take control of your day, manage your time, and get used to saying "no" when you are pulled in several directions at once. Take on what you can handle and delegate the rest. Set aside time to prioritize the most important people in your life.

When you are faced with a challenging situation, try to think of a positive quote or an inspirational statement and draw strength from it. Get over the moments when you make a mistake and move forward. Remember to take deep breaths or count to ten if you are presented with an opportunity to react to something unpleasant. Go for a walk or put on some relaxing music to calm your nerves. Find a hobby that takes your mind off your circumstance for a while. The point here is to be prepared and ready to make decisions under pressure. The last thing you want to do is something that will cost you a loss in the end. Develop a game plan and be aware of your weaknesses. Stay focused and don't let up.

How can you handle stress?

_____

_____

_____

_____

_____

_____

_____

_____

_____

_____

_____

_____

_____

_____

_____

_____

_____

_____

_____

_____

_____

_____

_____

_____

_____

_____

_____

_____

_____

WEEK 12 | ARE YOU DETERMINED TO BE BETTER?

Michelle Medlock Adams

LONGTIME IU BASKETBALL FANS FONDLY remember Landon Turner's hardwood contributions—he helped the Hoosiers secure the 1981 National Championship banner that flies high in Assembly Hall. Of course, fans also remember the horrific car accident that paralyzed Landon in July 1981. (See chapter 32 for more about that.) And some fans may remember that Turner spent a great deal of time in Coach Knight's doghouse his first two years at Indiana University.

Jim Crews, an IU assistant coach at the time, once described Turner: "He could be the most enjoyable player to coach and then the most frustrating." Turner's play was inconsistent his freshman and sophomore years, and his commitment to his education was also not cutting it with Coach Knight. But when Turner's junior year rolled around, the 6'10" powerhouse showed up, scoring 23 points against Notre Dame and Baylor. A more focused Turner started playing like Knight always knew he could—until inconsistency reared its ugly head again as Big Ten season got underway. Coach kept on Turner, telling him to take ownership of his play, and the big man responded by playing an essential role in Indiana's last five Big Ten wins.

During the press conference after IU beat Ohio State 74–58, Coach Knight said, "Turner has made great strides in that it upsets him to make mistakes. When it upsets a player to make mistakes, he's come a long way toward becoming a better player."[1]

I've read that quote by Coach Knight several times over the years, and it always causes me to stop and think. In other words, Turner had become so determined to play better that making mistakes upset him to his very core—he got so upset that he would work tirelessly to ensure he wouldn't make those same mistakes again.

When you're that passionate, success is on its way. You see, Turner's talent had always been there. He'd proven that with his stellar high school play, but during his first couple of years at IU, we saw only glimpses of that greatness. Still, Coach Knight knew it was within Turner and never gave up on him. Turner once told IndianaHQ.com that "Coach thought I could be the best player ever at IU, so when I didn't play like it, he just went off."[2]

BREAK THE PRESS

Sometimes in life, we need others to push us into greatness, and that's often very uncomfortable. Ask any woman who has gone through childbirth: pushing is the most painful part of labor and delivery, but the reward—the baby—makes it well worth the pain. It's the same in life. No matter how hard it gets, stay the course. Don't quit! Learn from your mistakes and don't be content with the status quo. Determine to be better. Anyone can just get by in life; it's only the person who pushes past the pain, listens to correction, and learns from past mistakes who achieves greatness.

So, let me ask you this: how badly do you want it?

SLAM DUNK

Do you find yourself coasting by in life, or are you always pressing toward excellence? Maybe it's time you step out of your comfort zone, stop settling for good enough, and go for greatness. Write down a list of people who have pushed you to be great. Why not send them a note this week to thank them for believing in you and nudging you down the path of success?

———————————————————————————————

———————————————————————————————

———————————————————————————————

NOTE

1. Chris Williams, "Hoosier Spotlight: Landon Turner," The Assembly Call, May 17, 2019, https://assemblycall.com/hoosier-spotlight-landon-turner/.

2. "Landon Turner," History, IndianaHQ, last modified September 30, 2019, https://indianahq.com/landon-turner/.

WEEK 13 | STAY FOCUSED

Del Duduit

On December 10, 2011, the unranked Indiana Hoosiers upset number-one ranked Kentucky Wildcats 73–72. Three weeks later, they upset the number-two team in the nation, the Buckeyes of Ohio State. With the win, IU became the ninth team since 1996–97 to defeat number-one and number-two teams in the same season. Kansas and Louisville were the only two other teams to have achieved such an accomplishment. It was Indiana's first-ever sweep of the top two teams in the country.

In the win over the Wildcats, Indiana needed a three-point buzzer beater by Christian Walford to be victorious. Three weeks later, the Hoosiers used an easy layup from Victor Oladipo, clutch free throws from Walford and Jordan Hull, and key defensive play—all in the final forty seconds—to pull off the upset win. The number-two ranked Buckeyes tried to pull away in the second half after they grabbed a 44–41 lead. But foul trouble and solid IU defense played a factor. The Hoosiers had their own players in foul trouble when Cody Zeller was whistled for his fifth on a play against Jared Sullinger that boosted the OSU lead to 68–67. Ohio State's Deshaun Thomas then connected on a bucket to put the Bucks ahead 70–68 with just under two minutes to play.

Moments later, Oladipo caught a pass from Verdell Jones off a defensive deflection by Hull and made the layup for the 71–70 lead with thirty-six ticks left on the clock. Hull and Watford sealed the deal with free throws. They did not let the road loss to Michigan State three nights earlier dampen their desire.

The Hoosiers accepted the challenge of playing the number-two team and beating them in Indiana style, just like they had when the Wildcats had gone down three weeks earlier. Indiana used a laser-like focus to find victory. There are many benefits to being focused on a mission.

BREAK THE PRESS

It's easy to become distracted in everyday life. You have a job with many responsibilities. You might have children and a family that keep you hopping. On top of that, perhaps you are involved in a few extracurricular activities, such as a softball league or a civic organization, that take up a lot of your time. And maybe you have a hobby, or you volunteer for a charity. There's an expression that says if you need something done, ask a person who is busy. There is little time to relax. At the same time, you can become distracted and lose focus on your goal. You can do only so much.

SLAM DUNK

Organization has its benefits, and I deal with this daily. I often misplace my glasses, my keys, and even my calendar. This is why my wife put an electronic finder inside my planner and on my keys. Life is hectic, and the last thing you need is to spend ten minutes searching for something you lost. When you are organized and focused on a goal, you feel more in control, confident, and positive. This will lead to better decision-making and increased clarity. Indiana's focus on their goal helped them to knock off the number-one and number-two ranked teams in the country in the same month. Imagine what it can do for you.

How can you become more focused? Can you become more organized?

_____

_____

_____

_____

WEEK 14 | IT'S THE HEART THAT MATTERS

Michelle Medlock Adams

DECEMBER 10, 2011: INDIANA 73, KENTUCKY 72

A bright star was born in the middle of five-star talent.

Kentucky entered Assembly Hall ranked number one in the nation. The Wildcats lineup featured talent like Anthony Davis, Michael Kidd-Gilchrist, and Marquise Teague. Kentucky stood as the favorite to win the championship in 2011.

On paper, the Hoosiers appeared outmatched, but sometimes heart matters more than talent. Hoosier star Victor Oladipo and freshman sensation Cody Zeller kept the Wildcats off-balance. When Will Sheehey hit a three in the second half, Indiana led by 10 points. IU proved that Kentucky wasn't going home with an easy win.

Assembly Hall rocked, but Kentucky responded. With under two minutes to play, the Wildcats led by one at 69–68. Indiana, trying to take a huge step in the rebuilding process, needed the win. A moral victory meant little. The lead changed hands twice. The Hoosiers led by number-one Kentucky answered to reclaim the lead.

Anthony Davis stepped to the line for a one-and-one with fifteen seconds to play. His miss gave Indiana another chance. A turnover forced Indiana to foul, leaving only six seconds on the clock. Doron Lamb hit one of two, offering the Hoosiers another shot to win. One final shot. Indiana fans held their collective breath.

Indiana raced down the court. Verdell Jones, aware of the clock, flipped the ball back to Christian Watford. The 6'9" junior let a three fly, shooting over a Kentucky defender flying at him. As the buzzer sounded, the ball swished through the net, and the crowd erupted. (I was on spring break in Florida, watching from a beach condo. My friends and I cheered so loudly, I thought we might get kicked out. As a former cheerleader, I actually sprang into a toe touch—which I regretted later. Still, it was the best victory ever!)

On paper, the talent advantage was in Kentucky's favor. But in the heart department and on the scoreboard, Indiana stood victorious. Do you have the heart of a champion beating inside of you? Are you willing to give life your all, knowing that those who are passionate about what they do are the most successful?

BREAK THE PRESS

Do you ever feel like you aren't enough? Are there times when you look around and feel like others are more talented, more gifted, or more successful than you? Others seem to complete with ease things that require much more effort from you. Comparing yourself to others is a dangerous game to play. Though others have talent, they may take it for granted. The greatest attribute a person holds cannot be seen with the eye. It's that intangible quality that turns a good player into a legend. And that same heart takes the ordinary to the extraordinary.

SLAM DUNK

In life, some things are simply out of your control. When you feel like you are a step behind others, you have the ability to try harder, work longer, and exceed even your own expectations. Heart is what makes real champions. Those who give their best efforts are true winners. Though some may rate your talent as subpar, you can reach greater heights with your effort and endurance. Commit yourself fully to what you are doing. Let your passion and your heart push you. Become the champion that already beats inside of you.

Do you believe you have the heart of a winner? Or do you feel that you aren't enough? What can you focus on when you feel like you are lacking? What will help you keep going?

_____

_____

_____

_____

_____

_____

_____

_____

_____

_____

_____

_____

_____

_____

_____

_____

_____

_____

_____

_____

_____

_____

_____

_____

_____

_____

_____

_____

_____

WEEK 15 | THE SWEET 16

Del Duduit

MARCH 17, 2012: INDIANA 63, VIRGINIA COMMONWEALTH 61

Over the past few years, Indiana and Coach Tom Crean had worked to make Hoosier basketball relevant again.

During the regular season, IU sent messages that it was back when the team knocked off number-one Kentucky and number-two Ohio State within three weeks. Now they were in the NCAA Big Dance, and the squad was playing well.

The Hoosiers defeated New Mexico State 79–66 in the first round of the tournament and faced Virginia Commonwealth University, a team that always played well in the field of sixty-eight over the years. The game, played in Portland, Oregon, was tense and hard-fought. With 23 seconds left to play, the contest was tied 61–61. The ball was passed inside and then kicked out to Will Sheehey on the baseline. He was used to clutch shots because he was the player who had nailed the game winner in the upset win over Kentucky earlier in the season.

This was no different. He was wide open and decided to take the shot while he could. *Swish.* Another bucket made with the game on the line. But the competition wasn't over yet. Twelve ticks were left on the clock. Indiana all-star forward Cody Zeller forced VCU guard Darius Theus not to take a shot and instead to pass the ball out to the top, where Rob Brandenberg hoisted a three-pointer. *Clunk!* Off the rim, and the Hoosiers won the game to send them to the Sweet 16 to face Kentucky.

Zeller was dominant in the last few minutes of the game. He finished with 16 points and 13 rebounds and altered several VCU shot attempts. Indiana fans had come to realize the journey Crean had brought them on was becoming real. Indiana Basketball was relevant once again. Hoosiermania was alive and well and back in the Big Dance.

Are you relevant? Does your opinion matter? Have you come back from a long dry spell?

BREAK THE PRESS

You might find yourself in a similar situation. For a few years, you have felt unimportant and useless in the eyes of the world. Maybe a major life event has set you back. Maybe you suffered a job loss and misplaced your identity. Perhaps a failed relationship left you bitter and hurt, and you felt alone and drifted away from friends and family. You have wandered by yourself long enough. It's time to turn your life around and get back in the game.

SLAM DUNK

No matter what you have battled, you must realize that your life is worth living. When you decide to come off the bench and onto the court, you need to make sure you don't take on too much at first. Pace yourself, get loose, and run up down the court a few times before you take that important shot. Develop and demonstrate a positive attitude and outlook. Few people enjoy being around someone who is negative and complains. Be uplifting. Make sure you get plenty of exercise and eat healthy because your energy is important. When you have some important decisions to make, consult with friends or take the time to weigh the pros and cons. An impulse can spell disaster. Make sure you take ownership of past mistakes and make a commitment to learn and never repeat the action. And remember to laugh and enjoy each day.

Another way to feel important is to volunteer and sacrifice your time for charity. This will help you see your situation in a different light and help others at the same time. Manage your stress level and adopt a thankful attitude. Make amends with those you have wronged, and work to build up your self-esteem.

Remember it took Crean about four years to bring the Hoosiers back to contention. Your journey will be long, so pace yourself and cherish each day.

How will you become relevant again?

_____

_____

_____

_____

_____

_____

_____

_____

_____

_____

_____

_____

_____

_____

_____

_____

_____

_____

_____

_____

_____

_____

_____

_____

_____

_____

_____

_____

_____

_____

_____

WEEK 16 | SILENCE THE CRITICS

Michelle Medlock Adams

MARCH 21, 2002: INDIANA 74, DUKE 73

Disrespect drives an underdog. Duke learned such a lesson in the 2002 NCAA tournament.

In Mike Davis's second year at the helm, he led the team to nineteen wins in the regular season and a five-seed in the NCAA tournament. After dismantling Utah and UNC-Wilmington on the first weekend, Indiana moved on to the Sweet 16 for the first time since the 1993–94 season.

As the Hoosiers and the Blue Devils prepared for a Sweet 16 matchup, a Duke administrator's comments fueled the Hoosiers' fire. The individual from Duke asked what time the Blue Devils would play on Saturday, dismissing Indiana's chances of winning on Thursday night. At the Wednesday night meeting, Coach Mike Davis heard the comment and relayed the message to his team. The Hoosiers became an underdog on a mission to prove the critics wrong. Though they were 13-point underdogs, disrespect drove them to go after the Blue Devils with everything they had.

Duke, the defending national champions, held a 13-point halftime lead. The Hoosiers had twenty minutes to dig in and prove the critics wrong or go home. Jared Jeffries, A. J. Moye, and Jarrad Odle led, as the determined guys from Bloomington fought back. A spirited second-half comeback put the Hoosiers in a position to win. Indiana executed while the Blue Devils faltered down the stretch. Moye's spinning shot in the lane had the Hoosiers within six and believing. Then Jeffries made a big rebound and put it back up, cutting the deficit to one.

Duke rebuilt the lead to six. Indiana clawed back. When Tom Cloverdale tied the game with free throws at 70–70, the critics and oddsmakers swallowed a collective lump in their throats. Cloverdale's first field goal gave the Hoosiers their first lead with fifty-six seconds remaining.

Indiana held on in the frantic final seconds and pulled off an upset that still gives me chills. Rather than playing on Saturday, as the Duke administrator had assumed, the Blue Devils sat in Durham and watched Indiana advance to the Final Four. #iknowthatsright

Do you allow the voices of critics to hinder you, or do those voices push you to success? Are you ready to prove your critics wrong?

BREAK THE PRESS

Criticism abounds in our world today. Do you make decisions based upon the words of a critic? Have you allowed negative criticism or disrespect to stop you? Sometimes, it's hard to drown out the negative voices, so use them to motivate you. Fear of criticism prevents many from experiencing greater things in life. There will always be those who say you can't. The question is . . . will you listen to them?

SLAM DUNK

Let the critics drive you to success. Words have the power to defeat or to motivate. When someone tries to stop you with their doubts, believe in yourself enough to keep pushing forward. As Theodore Roosevelt once said, the critic isn't the one who matters. No, it's the person who gets in the arena, the one who puts it all on the line to achieve something great—that's the person who matters. Be that person! And surround yourself with people who will support you and celebrate with you when success comes.

Go out today and prove the critics wrong. The world may see you as an underdog, but the only thing that matters is how you see yourself. Get your winner's eyes in focus and see yourself as a victor!

How can you use the criticism and skeptics to push you toward accomplishing your goals in life?

_____

_____

_____

_____

_____

_____

_____

_____

_____

_____

_____

_____

_____

_____

_____

_____

_____

_____

_____

_____

_____

_____

_____

_____

_____

_____

_____

_____

_____

WEEK 17 | MAMA KNOWS BEST

Michelle Medlock Adams

ISIAH THOMAS

A couple of expressions come to mind when talking about mothers. One: "If mama ain't happy, ain't nobody happy." And two: "Mama's always right." I bet if you asked Isiah Thomas about those two expressions, he'd agree . . . especially with the latter one. You see, if it hadn't been for Mary Thomas, Isiah would not have ended up at Indiana University. (Can you even imagine IU Basketball history without Isiah Thomas in it?)

In a podcast interview with Quentin Richardson and Darius Miles, Isiah shared that he had planned to go to DePaul, where he could play for the highly successful Blue Demons alongside his friends Mark Aguirre and Terry Cummings. Plus, DePaul was only about twenty miles away from Isiah's hometown. DePaul was the plan until Coach Bob Knight made a visit to the Thomas household, and he didn't come alone. He came with Wayne Embry and Quinn Buckner. As Isiah tells it, Coach Knight didn't even talk to him during the recruiting visit; he talked directly with Isiah's mama.

It was no secret that pretty much everyone wanted Isiah Thomas to play for them, and some were even willing to offer money to make that happen—lots of money. But Mary Thomas flat-out rejected the monetary offers, stating that her son was not for sale. When Coach Knight and company came to recruit Isiah, he was just one of many coaches making a play for her son. But Coach didn't come to play. He came to win.

As Isiah tells it, Knight didn't make any promises he couldn't keep, and he didn't make them to Isiah. He made them to Mama Thomas.

"I'll never forget, he said I'm going to offer you and your son three things," Isiah remembered. "He is going to be a gentlemen. I'll teach him everything that I know about basketball. And he'll get a great education."[1]

That was all Mary needed to hear. While Isiah wasn't thrilled with his mama's decision, he went along with the press conference that she called announcing to the world that her baby boy had decided to attend IU. After all, Mama's always right, right?

The rest, as they say, is history. Isiah ended up loving his days at Indiana University, especially the time he spent playing for Coach Knight. And Isiah made his mark during his abbreviated time at IU, cut short because he ended up going pro after only one year. Those collegiate accolades included being named to the Associated Press All-Big Ten team in 1980 (the first college freshman to receive that honor) and leading the Hoosiers to the 1981 NCAA basketball championship as well as being named tournament MVP.

Going to IU proved to be the right decision, even though Isiah didn't think so at the time. Thank God for wise mamas who give wise counsel.

Have you thanked your mama or the person in your life who has offered you advice and made the hard decisions where you're concerned? Or maybe you're the parent in that position, giving counsel and making the tough calls on behalf of your children. That can feel like a thankless job sometimes, can't it? Well, listen to your heart. Stand your ground. And do your best for the people in your life.

BREAK THE PRESS

Has there ever been a time in your life when a loved one gave you advice you didn't like? How did you handle that advice? Did you take it under advisement, or did you reject it immediately? Part of growing up and growing wiser is learning to receive counsel—even when you totally disagree with it.

SLAM DUNK

Here's the thing about advice from someone who loves you: even if you don't agree with it, you have to believe that it comes from a good place.

With that in mind, listen to the advice and take it under consideration. Yes, mamas are usually right, but so are others in your circle of influence. If you choose not to adhere to anyone else's counsel, you might find yourself in dangerous territory. Ever heard the expression "pride comes before a fall"? By being too prideful to accept input from those you love and respect, you risk stunting your growth and possibly missing out on amazing opportunities.

How can you become more receptive to advice from those in your circle?

_____

_____

_____

_____

_____

_____

_____

_____

_____

_____

_____

_____

_____

_____

_____

_____

_____

_____

_____

_____

_____

_____

NOTE

1. Mike Schumann, "IU Basketball: How Isiah Thomas' Mom Delivered the Hoosiers' 1981 National Title," *The Daily Hoosier*, May 6, 2020, https://www.thedailyhoosier.com/iu -basketball-how-isiah-thomas-mom-delivered-the-hoosiers-1981-national-title/.

WEEK 18 | YOUR ONE SHINING MOMENT

Michelle Medlock Adams

MARCH 30, 1987: INDIANA 74, SYRACUSE 73

After missing a shot in the final minute, the amazing athlete from Baton Rouge, Louisiana, ran down the court, a championship moment awaiting.

Keith Smart, the guard with a forty-two-inch vertical leap, along with Steve Alford, kept the Hoosiers in the game during tough stretches. Smart had 15 points in the second half, but after Syracuse took a 1-point lead, Smart missed a jumper that would have given the Hoosiers the lead.

But that wasn't the end of his story. Though Syracuse regained possession, they missed their free throws, giving the Hoosiers one more shot. Alford could have taken the shot. He was 7-10 from three-point range for the game. The ball in Daryl Thomas's hands made sense as well. Thomas had scored 20 points in the game, showing he wasn't afraid of the bright lights.

As time ran down, Smart swung the ball toward the baseline. A swarming Syracuse defense forced the ball to be reversed, back in the hands of the one who had missed the previous chance to secure the lead. Without hesitation and with a dribble to his left, he broke from the defender. Rising high in the Superdome, he stroked the jumper with three seconds remaining. An iconic image emerged as the ball swished through the net.

Smart, who had transferred to Indiana from Garden City Community College, wanted to play big-time basketball. With one shot, he was immortalized in the game forever. Focused on sealing the game, Smart intercepted Syracuse's full-court pass, cementing the outcome for the Hoosier Nation. What a shot! What a day! What a moment in Indiana University Basketball history!

Amazingly, 1987 was the first year CBS used the song "One Shining Moment." It had originally been planned for the Super Bowl, but the Super Bowl broadcast ran long, so the song was cut and passed along to the college basketball championship. The last image in the montage from the 1987 tournament was Keith Smart's shot, as the song plays, "One shining moment. It's all on the line. One shining moment, there frozen in time."

Smart's moment was history-making in multiple ways.

Could today be the day for you to make history? Does this day hold the opportunity for your shining moment?

BREAK THE PRESS

A missed opportunity, a setback, or a mistake can make you leery of stepping up when a moment arrives. What if you fail? What if others see you fall short? The embarrassment of failing causes many to pass the ball in life rather than take the shot. They'd rather be forgotten than be remembered for failing. Frozen in fear, they miss opportunities, and memories are not made. Maybe you fell short before, and the fear of doing it again keeps you from embracing that one shining moment. Remember, somebody has to take the last shot. Let that somebody be you!

SLAM DUNK

Your moment stands before you. You have a chance for greatness, so step up and take the shot. The dream of success becomes a reality only when you do the work and then recognize those moments designed for you to shine. Rather than hope for another shot, take the one that is before you today. Forget any shot that you took in the past that bounced off the rim, and see that this time, you can make a mark on the world.

No one who tries, who risks it all for greatness, is a failure. Willingness and bravery are two key elements to making history, and you have those traits. Dig down deep—they are in you. Take your shot today so you don't look back later with regret.

What is the winning shot you need to take in your life today? Better yet, what is stopping you?

_____

_____

_____

_____

_____

_____

_____

_____

_____

_____

_____

_____

_____

_____

_____

_____

_____

_____

_____

_____

_____

_____

_____

_____

_____

_____

_____

_____

WEEK 19 | FIND A SILVER LINING

Del Duduit

There have been better seasons in the storied history of Indiana Basketball than 1962. The Hoosiers finished 13-11 under head coach Branch McCracken and 9-5 in the Big Ten Conference. It was below expectations to say the least.

But in every situation, look for the positives. Although these moments don't change the outcome, they can instill hope and encouragement in otherwise dismal moments. This was the case on January 27, 1962. Indiana entered the conference game against the Golden Gophers 7-5. The season was not what fans had hoped for up to this point.

But Jimmy Rayl put on a performance that left everyone with a big smile. The "Mr. Basketball" of 1959 lit up the scoreboard and poured in 56 points, setting a new single-game Big Ten record. He not only sent the game into overtime, but he banged home a thirty-foot shot at the buzzer to win the game for the Hoosiers. When it was all over, he had scored 20 of the final 22 points.

Jimmy put on this amazing performance during a time when the 3-point shot did not exist. He made six field goals from more than twenty-five feet away from the basket, which would have put him at 62 points today.

When the long season ended, the Hoosiers were just above the .500 mark. But Jimmy posted a 29.8 points per game average and was named All-American and First Team All-Big Ten.

Are you going through a tough time? Sometimes it's difficult to find the silver lining, but keep looking.

BREAK THE PRESS

Maybe you're going through a job layoff, or a person you love has some health issues. Perhaps you have a relationship with a family member that could be better. You might be facing a decision that could change your family's life forever. Or perhaps you're struggling to find a solid job and did not picture your life turning out like it has.

There are many scenarios that could bring you down. But you have to establish a game plan and come out to play each minute of the game with the right attitude.

SLAM DUNK

No matter the situation, keep shooting. You can't win the game unless you take shots at the goal. Don't be a ball hog and force shots when they're not there, but rely on the picks and screens from your teammates to get open looks at the basket. You must be a team player, and the goal is to work together to win the game.

Your handling of uncomfortable situations will reveal your character. View change as an opportunity to start anew. Accept the challenge and be grateful for the chance to embark on an adventure. Use your experience to develop a game plan and be an encouragement to others.

Jimmy's performance was the good that came out of an average season for Indiana Basketball. Fans still talk about the game when his shot at the buzzer proved victorious.

They may not recall the season—but they do remember the way he played. This was the silver lining. You can find one too.

How can you adapt and change your attitude to find the good in a bad situation?

_____

_____

_____

_____

WEEK 20 | WHEN A GAME IS MORE THAN A GAME

Michelle Medlock Adams

DECEMBER 4, 1948: INDIANA 61, DEPAUW 48

A season-opening game in 1948 was more than a game. A decision broke an unwritten rule and brought change in the game that was long overdue.

Branch McCracken sent his five starters out to face DePauw. One of them, Bill Garrett, was African American. For the Hoosiers and the Big Ten Conference, Garrett's presence in the starting lineup led to a new day. His regular presence throughout the season spoke of a new beginning. Though Dick Culbertson appeared in a game for Iowa as a substitute player, Garrett's role shattered the old way of thinking.

Indiana rolled to an opening-season win, but the game meant much more than a W in the win column. Coach McCracken started a movement against injustice. Bill Garrett contributed to the victory, both on the court and off the court. In the game, he scored 8 points for the Hoosiers. He averaged 10 points per game his first season, leading the team in scoring. Off the court, his impact extended further. Garrett played with courage as the Hoosiers traveled from school to school, often the target of taunting, racial statements and angry fans. His toughest battles, however, were with opponents and critics off the court. Still, he stood up and endured the persecution for the sake of those who would follow him.

Together, Garrett and McCracken blazed a trail in the Big Ten. By the 1951–52 season, seven African Americans played on varsity teams in the Big Ten.

McCracken saw an injustice, so he fought for what was right regardless of whether it was popular at the moment. He stood by Garrett, and together they changed history.

When you see injustice in the world around you, how do you react?

BREAK THE PRESS

What will people say? If we're all honest, that question comes to our minds more often than we'd like to admit. Situations stand before you. The world offers a steady diet of wrongs as well as injustices each day. Some are minor wrongs that need to be addressed while others are egregious and demand attention. Many feel there is little option other than to comply with popular thinking. After all, speaking out can lead to persecution. True, speaking up may leave you outcast, but if not you, who? Who will be the voice for the voiceless?

This is the very season when leaders are needed. A true leader is more than the holder of a title or position—a true leader acts upon the sight of injustice and confronts the problem. Are you that leader?

SLAM DUNK

In a world desperate for leadership, seize the opportunity that is before you. True leadership is based on doing what is right, not what is popular. People need to see others stepping up, and you can lead the way! Have courage. Take action. When you see a wrong, speak up and step up. Though everyone has opinions, few have enough conviction to do anything. This is your chance to make a difference by turning the tide rather than turning a cold shoulder.

What injustices do you see around you, and what actions can you take to lead the change?

_____

_____

_____

_____

_____

_____

WEEK 21 | TAKING DOWN A GIANT

Michelle Medlock Adams

MARCH 21, 1992: INDIANA 89, LSU 79

When the brackets are released, teams see the obstacles standing between themselves and the Final Four. For the 1992 Hoosiers, Selection Sunday revealed a potential giant in the way.

Shaquille O'Neal and the LSU Tigers awaited the Hoosiers after Indiana blasted past Eastern Illinois in the first round. From the opening tip, the Hoosiers proved they were not afraid. A giant in the way meant a giant needed to be slayed.

On their first possession, Damon Bailey, the 6'3" guard, drove right at the 7'1" center. Though the floater careened off the rim, Bailey made a statement. On the second possession, the Hoosiers again stormed the lane. Though LSU powered its way to an early 14-point lead at 27–13, Indiana collectively kept fighting. When O'Neal sat for a rest, the Hoosiers took the momentum away from the Tigers and closed the half on a 32–11 run.

LSU fought to keep the game close in the second half, but the Hoosiers' teamwork proved to be too much. O'Neal had a monster game, scoring 36 points while hauling in 12 rebounds. However, the Hoosiers, with four players in double figures, led by Calbert Cheaney's 30 points, took down a giant.

A 10-point victory sent Indiana to the Sweet 16 and ended the collegiate career of Shaquille O'Neal. Coach Bob Knight, the fearless leader, instilled fearlessness in his players. Even in the face of a man the size of Shaquille O'Neal, the Hoosiers stuck together and were unshaken.

Are you surrounded by others who are fighting for the same goals? Do you have a team around you that is committed to success?

BREAK THE PRESS

Are you facing giants in your life today? Do you feel like you're facing them alone, hoping to muster up enough inside yourself to make it past the obstacles before you?

Giants come in all areas of life. Maybe the situation you face today is in your career. You want to take the next step but cannot do it on your own. Could it be that the giant is a health situation that you shudder to face alone? Financial, mental, emotional, and relational giants threaten our safety and our sanity. Times arise when our giants are the voices inside ourselves, the constant taunting from within that says we are not enough. Those imposing realities can overwhelm us, or they can become part of our stories of triumph. The greatest stories ever told are of those who stand up, fight on, and overcome. Your story waits to be told. Now is the time to assemble the right team around you.

SLAM DUNK

A great team is composed of various talents striving together for the same goal. Take an honest look at those you consider to be on your team. Find the voices that encourage you rather than discourage you. We need cheerleaders and teammates. Choose to join forces with those whose hands help you up and help you out rather than hands that only hold you back and push you down. With the help of the right team, you can slay any giant that stands in the way of you achieving your goals in life. See the giant for what it is—a momentary interruption along life's journey.

Who are the most essential members of your life's team, and what makes them indispensable? Conversely, what giants are standing in the way of your dreams becoming a reality?

_____

_____

_____

WEEK 22 | TEAMWORK ALWAYS WINS

Del Duduit

FEBRUARY 28, 2012: INDIANA 70, MICHIGAN STATE 55

The number-five ranked Spartans rolled into Bloomington late in the season to face off with the number-eighteen ranked Hoosiers. Michigan State was 24-5 and 13-3 in the Big Ten and ran into an Indiana buzz saw. But it took a total team effort to knock off Tim Izzo's squad 304 miles to the north.

Cody Zeller poured in 18 points while Victor Oladipo added 13; Christian Watford chipped in 10 and added 14 rebounds in the win. On the other end, Michigan State's Draymond Green—the best player in the conference, many experts speculated—scored 29 points to lead his team, including 16 straight in one 12-minute stretch. However, no other Spartan scored more than 8 points. While three Hoosiers combined to score 41 points in the win, Green did not receive complementary support from his team.

Indiana was better in all aspects of the game. They rebounded more aggressively and played determined defense. Their passing game was crisp, and their shot selection was calculated. The Hoosiers, who improved to 23-7 and 10-7, whooped the Spartans and knocked off the third team ranked in the top five for the season, the first squad to pull off an accomplishment like this since 1948–49.

The win was Indiana's best team performance of the season, just days before the Big Ten tournament was set to begin. Indiana joined Kansas as the only teams to upset three teams ranked in the top five in 2011. But it took teamwork.

Do you pull your weight on the job or at home? Can your teammates count on you to contribute?

BREAK THE PRESS

What would you do in the following situation? You've worked hard all week, and it's been a tough one. You stayed up late a few nights getting a report ready for an important presentation. Many obstacles distracted you, such as a flat tire. Your youngest child was sick for a few days, and your internet went on the fritz. Still, you stayed focused and took care of business.

Now the weekend is here, and all you want to do is play some golf with your buddies. The forecast is perfect, and the tee time is set. You've looked forward to this all week and need to recharge. But just before you place your golf bag in the car, your wife lets you know she is now feeling under the weather. She needs your help with the laundry and dishes. She had also planned to run several errands and take your daughter to a birthday party.

What will you do? Will you be a team player or one that seeks to score all the points and loses the game?

SLAM DUNK

Although the decision is not hard, it does place you in a difficult situation. You've anticipated that first tee shot and spending time with the guys. On the other hand, your wife needs your help. After all, she works hard too. But more importantly, your entire family depends on you to come through. Spending time on yourself must take a back seat. Your family—your team—must come first. Don't lose focus and have a bad attitude about lending a hand. The clothes need to be cleaned, and the birthday party is important to your child.

When you put yourself last and others first, you are a winner in any book. The Hoosiers found this out when they knocked off a number-five ranked team. They did not do this with one athlete; instead, they relied on the entire squad. Your team needs you to step up and deliver.

How can you be a team player at home or at work?

_____

_____

_____

_____

_____

_____

_____

_____

_____

_____

_____

_____

_____

_____

_____

_____

_____

_____

_____

_____

_____

_____

_____

_____

_____

_____

_____

_____

_____

_____

_____

_____

WEEK 23 | A LIGHT AT THE END OF THE TUNNEL

Michelle Medlock Adams

JANUARY 7, 2001: INDIANA 59, MICHIGAN STATE 58

Engulfed in the darkness of Bobby Knight's dismissal in September, the Hoosiers needed a ray of light.

The start of the season had been rocky. A three-game skid had concluded with a loss to rival Indiana State. By January 7, Indiana's record was 9-6, and an ominous cloud hung over the program.

Michigan State entered Assembly Hall as the top-ranked team in the nation as well as the defending national champions. MSU's winning streak stood at twenty-three games. The matchup looked uneven, but, as any loyal IU fan knows, matchups on paper have little to do with heart.

The Hoosiers needed a spark. Fans were desperate for a glimmer of hope. As the Spartans led 46–40 in the second half, Kirk Haston hit a three to ignite a 9–0 Hoosiers scoring run. However, his biggest shot came late in the game. Michigan State reclaimed the lead, and as the clock wound down, the Spartans had opportunities to seal the game. Yet the Spartans' inability to execute the fundamentals proved costly and gave Indiana a chance.

In the final thirty seconds, Michigan State missed three of four free throws. Indiana inbounded the ball with roughly seven seconds left. The ball swung around the top of the key until it reached Haston. A dribble to his left created separation, and fast as lightning, he pulled the trigger on a deep three. The ball hung in the air as the anticipation built. The horn sounded as the ball whooshed through the net, sending Assembly Hall into a frenzy. The fans spilled onto the court. Coach Davis broke down in front of the bench. A shot pierced the night that had fallen on IU Basketball four months earlier. A reason to celebrate reminded the Hoosiers that the program could recover after the tumultuous times. Basketball again brought tears of joy.

Though life assures times of darkness, do you see the light piercing through?

BREAK THE PRESS

A season of turmoil in life overwhelms you. One wave crashes after another. Darkness expands to the point of suffocation as hopelessness threatens. Each day seems to bring a new concern, and thoughts of what could unravel next makes for sleepless nights. Whether you're dealing with job difficulties, financial troubles, broken relationships, or health issues, hang in there. Though the night seems long, joy comes in the morning. That's a promise. Don't allow fear and hopelessness to take up residence in your heart. The darkness will pass. Better days are on the horizon if you'll just hold on to hope and keep believing in a brighter tomorrow.

SLAM DUNK

Your focus often dictates your perspective. If you only stare at the problems, you will feel defeated. The scenarios of what could unfold rob you of your energy and steal your attention throughout the day. If you choose to focus on those little appearances of light, the small things that go right, you will be empowered to keep pushing forward. Unexpected victories propel you and inspire you. Even small triumphs are reminders that better days are ahead. Rather than give up, look up and see the sun shining. Your best days are coming.

How does focusing on the positives help you during difficult times? What positives can you focus on today?

_____

_____

_____

WEEK 24 | GET THE MONKEY OFF YOUR BACK

Del Duduit

NOVEMBER 28, 2011: INDIANA 75, BUTLER 59

The Butler Bulldogs and the Purdue Boilermakers were both trying to dethrone the Hoosiers as the basketball kings of the state of Indiana. Butler had made significant runs in the NCAA tournament while Purdue was dominating the Big Ten conference. For the past decade, the two schools had grabbed all the headlines and recognition the Hoosiers were previously accustomed to receiving. Could Coach Tom Crean keep up with the pace set by Brad Stevens of Butler and Matt Painter of Purdue?

Indiana hosted the Hoosier Invitational in November 2011, and Butler came into the game riding a ten-year high of solid basketball performance. The Bulldogs came out blazing, but Indiana withstood a huge challenge and knocked them off 75–59, thanks in part to a Will Sheehey 21-point performance off the bench. The small forward from Stuart, Florida, was named tournament MVP in the round-robin tournament that featured Butler, Savannah State, Chattanooga, and Gardner Webb along with Indiana.

Sheehey connected on five of eight shots from the field and swished eight of ten attempts from the free-throw line. He also hit three from three-point land in four tries. He was on target. The Hoosiers went 4-0 in the tournament to claim the title and boosted their overall record to 6-0 at the time.

The win helped get the monkey off Crean's back and assured the fans at Indiana that he was the man for the job. Indiana faithful were beginning to witness a rebirth of Hoosier hysteria. And it all started with Sheehey coming off the bench to do his job. He wasn't fancy, but he got the job done.

What is your monkey? Is there something in your life that weighs you down?

BREAK THE PRESS

The monkey can be anything that keeps you up at night. You might struggle with a personal addiction or a bad habit you know must be broken. Maybe you fight temptation each day or you are in a difficult relationship that you wish were better. Your monkey could be a challenging boss at work or the financial problems we all encounter at times. The monkey may seem daunting and hard to catch, but you can come to grips and develop a winning game plan.

SLAM DUNK

No matter the monkey, you can be successful in getting him off your back. No challenge is too large to overcome, and no primate is too big to kick to the curb. You are not dealing with King Kong, but if you were, recall he is always killed in the end. One way to deal with the monkey is to be aware of the situation at hand. You must manage your emotions and respond appropriately. Don't let your feelings dictate your response because that could lead to something you might regret.

Another way to cope with unpleasant problems is to name your monkey. When you can identify the situation, it will be easier to deal with. When you know your opponent, you can identify its weakness. Crean studied game films of Butler and devised a way to beat them. Know what you're up against and don't be afraid. Don't feel sorry for yourself if the problem seems too big; instead, take an approach filled with confidence and manage the game. Remember there are four quarters, so don't give up if you're down early in the game.

When Indiana finally knocked off Butler, Crean felt more at ease and could focus on the season at hand much easier. Winning does wonders for self-esteem.

How will you get the monkey off your back?

_____

_____

_____

_____

_____

_____

_____

_____

_____

_____

_____

_____

_____

_____

_____

_____

_____

_____

_____

_____

_____

_____

_____

_____

_____

_____

_____

_____

WEEK 25 | HEALTHY RIVALRIES

Michelle Medlock Adams

WHEN YOU THINK OF SPIRITED sports rivalries, particularly in college basketball, who comes to mind? While many great college basketball rivalries exist, these are probably the most famous: Duke and North Carolina; Cincinnati and Xavier; Kentucky and Louisville; Michigan and Michigan State; Kansas and Kansas State; UCLA and Arizona; and Georgetown and Villanova. But the rivalry nearest and dearest to a Hoosier's heart has to be Indiana versus Purdue.

Separated by just over one hundred miles in a state that considers college basketball a religion, IU and Purdue have a very rich rivalry. Both are staples of the Big Ten, and both have bragging rights of sorts. Some sports analysts argue that Purdue is superior simply based on wins and losses. As it stands today, Purdue leads 122 to 89, touting 33 more wins than IU. Other sports gurus have declared IU the winner of this rivalry because Indiana has outperformed Purdue in NCAA tournament play. As it stands, the Boilermakers have made it to the Final Four only twice while IU has won five national championships.

The winner of this long-standing rivalry depends on the day and whom you ask, but one thing is for sure: there are some iconic IU versus Purdue moments that put the exclamation mark on the sentence "IU and Purdue will always be bitter enemies!" Let's revisit a couple.

The 1981 Incident (IU 69, Purdue 61)

Remember when IU's star Isiah Thomas came to blows with the Boilermakers' Roosevelt Barnes in a scuffle that didn't result in a single foul? Coach Knight later came to Isiah's defense by devoting his entire Sunday night TV show to the incident, showing game film to prove his point—that Barnes had been physical with Isiah first. Purdue and the press had commented over and over again since the incident that Isiah had sucker punched Barnes, never sharing that Barnes had clearly shoved or punched Isiah in the chin just moments earlier. Talk about fueling the rivalry fire.

The 1979 NIT Final (IU 53, Purdue 52)

Okay, it wasn't the Big Dance, but the NIT was still important, and IU wanted to win. It was a matchup of IU's Ray Tolbert and Purdue's Joe Barry Carroll, and neither team could pull away with any kind of lead. With just six seconds left on the clock, Butch Carter connected on the game-winning shot from the top of the key. It was sweet to win the NIT, but it was even sweeter to beat Purdue for that title.

No matter if both teams are ranked or having the worst season ever, when it's game time for IU versus Purdue, you can bet both teams will bring their A game. They will show up to play and usually give their best performance of the year in front of packed, very loud arenas. Why is that? Because rivalries often drive us to perform better.

Do you have a rivalry or a friendly foe who keeps you striving for excellence?

BREAK THE PRESS

The dictionary defines rivalry as "competition for the same objective or for superiority in the same field." Anytime you're striving to be the best in your field and you battle the same talented competitor year after year to be top dog, a rivalry will develop. It's human nature, and it's healthy. This happens in sports, families, and work.

I have more than one hundred books published at this point, and I participate in a sort of writing rivalry. You see, I not only write non-fiction books for adults, but I also write children's books and I often find them as contenders for "best children's book of the year" in various writers' contests. I've been fortunate and have won more than seventy industry awards over the years, but I've noticed that I am almost always competing with the same three to five children's writers. So, of course, I look for their books and study what they do so I can know my competition and glean information from their expertise. That's what makes it healthy. I learn more. I get better. I try harder. Who in your life pushes you to do the same?

SLAM DUNK

Some people are satisfied with the status quo, happy just to get by, okay with placing but never winning—but that's not how Indiana basketball teams approach the game. If they did, I'm pretty sure the Hoosier Nation would be more like a small Hoosier township. The fans demand excellence of their beloved Hoosiers. But fans should demand that same excellence of themselves—in how they represent the university and treat the players, coaches, opposing teams, and other fans. Rivalries are fun, and for the most part they are a healthy part of competition, but they can become heated and detrimental if taken too far. So, keep it fun. And keep striving for excellence in every area of your life.

Do you struggle to stay motivated? Who in your life pushes you to improve?

_____

_____

_____

_____

_____

_____

_____

_____

_____

_____

_____

_____

_____

_____

IU PLAYERS

WEEK 26 | FOLLOW YOUR HEART

Del Duduit

The hype was noticed and well-earned.

In November 2005, Eric Gordon announced his plans to play for the University of Illinois. He made this public yet unofficial announcement during his sophomore year in high school, much to the pleasure of Jim Weber, the coach of the Fighting Illini. Indiana fans were disappointed because many had hoped the North Central High School (Indianapolis) star would opt to stay close to home and play for the Hoosiers.

Three months later, Indiana head coach Mike Davis said he planned to resign after the 2005–06 season. In March 2006, Kelvin Sampson was hired to lead IU Basketball, which sparked Eric's attention. To make the situation even more interesting, Sampson brought Jeff Meyer on board to be part of his staff. Meyer had previously coached Eric's father and was a longtime family friend of the Gordons.

Since Gordon had not signed an official letter of intent, he could still be recruited and showed interest in playing for Indiana. By mid-July 2006, the race was on to see who could convince Eric to play for them. But Gordon reassured Illinois fans and coaches he intended to play for Weber.

When the 2006–07 season rolled around, Gordon was a high school senior sensation. He was a McDonald's All-American and was named Mr. Basketball in Indiana. In September 2006, he made an unofficial visit to Bloomington and scrimmaged with Hoosier basketball players. Two months later, on November 8, 2006, he made it official and signed a letter of intent to play for Indiana.

Hoosier fans and coaches were elated while Illinois fans felt like they were stood up at the prom. Many of them claimed that Indiana's recruitment was unethical because Gordon had made a verbal commitment and then changed his mind. But Sampson had done nothing wrong. Illinois fans and coaches were justifiably upset because the state's best player followed his heart.

When Gordon played in Champaign, Illinois, he and his family were booed and harassed by frustrated fans. But that was expected. He went on to have a marvelous season at Indiana and led the Big Ten in scoring with 21.5 points per game as a freshman. After his first year, he entered the NBA draft and was selected in the first round by the Los Angeles Clippers.

Although some people were not as understanding as they could have been, Gordon made the decision that was best for him. Should he have committed so early? Maybe not. But he made a choice and stayed with it for his benefit.

Have you ever been in a situation where you needed to change your mind?

BREAK THE PRESS

Choices. We make them every day. Most of them don't have life-changing results. You might not put much thought into deciding what to wear for the day or where to buy gasoline to save a few bucks. But how do you react when presented with options that can impact your life?

Have you ever made a decision and then thought, "What have I done?" We all have. Perhaps you made a choice in haste or had motivations that seemed reasonable at the time. But after more information presented itself, you had second thoughts. Maybe your boss offered you a promotion that could take your family away from people they love. Or perhaps you were influenced to select a destination for college, and your gut said no, but your friends said yes.

What did you do?

SLAM DUNK

Maybe you made a premature announcement to a large crowd and are now having second thoughts. Or you were presented with a decision you needed to make but have had some time to ponder, and now you're reconsidering. The last thing you want to do is make a harsh choice and tell everyone you know about it. The best thing you can do is trust your initial gut reaction. Follow that by dismissing all the negative thoughts and feelings that might follow. Make sure you confide in close friends and family and solicit and listen to their opinions—don't allow them to make the choice but ask them to participate in a discussion. Always weigh the pros and cons. Don't allow glamour or glory to persuade any decision. Then make your choice and face the consequences.

Be confident in who you are and what choices you make. Make them for the right reasons. Never allow pride to dictate a wrong path. Be strong enough to realize a mistake was made, change course, and move forward with the right one.

What are some factors that can change your mind? Be open to them.

_____

_____

_____

_____

_____

_____

_____

_____

_____

_____

_____

_____

_____

_____

_____

_____

_____

_____

WEEK 27 | MOUNTAINTOPS AND VALLEYS

Michelle Medlock Adams

KENT BENSON, INDIANA'S MR. BASKETBALL in 1973, was a force to be reckoned with when he donned his number 54 jersey at IU. Here are just a few of the accolades he earned while at IU: 1976 Consensus first-team All-American, 1976 Helms Foundation Player of the Year, 1976 NCAA Final Four Most Outstanding Player, a 1976 NCAA Champion, a three time All-Big Ten pick, and the 1977 league MVP.

Growing up, I just knew him as the redhead with the lethal hook shot. I admired him then, but the more I learned about Benson's time at IU, the more I respected this homegrown Hoosier. Benson's sheer physical power and his positive attitude were important contributions to the multitalented teams that together compiled an impressive 63-1 record from 1974 to 1976.

Can you imagine playing for those teams? What a high! But as you know, everything that goes up must come down. When Benson came back for his senior year, he was the only returning starter, with eight new underclassmen to round out the roster. Still, the team had a number-five preseason ranking based on IU's former success—*former* being the keyword in that sentence—because the 1977 season was not a storybook one. Benson did his best to lead, but the rest of the team's inexperience proved too much. IU finished 9-9 in conference play and did not get the chance to play in a postseason tournament. (That was the first and only season in Coach Knight's IU career that his team didn't play in a post-season tourney.) It was a tough senior year for Benson and probably not the way he had envisioned it, but he still played hard every single time he took the floor, which explains why he was chosen as Big Ten's Player of the Year. Coach Knight had this to say about Benson after his final game at IU: "His career more than anything epitomizes just what I would want an Indiana basketball player to be. I thought he started the season as the best center in the country and that's exactly the way he ended it."[1] That's high praise from The General.

It's no surprise Benson was a number-one draft pick that year and ended up playing eleven seasons in the NBA. I believe if he would have thrown in the towel of frustration his senior year after coming off the two-year mountaintop experience, he wouldn't have been chosen for the NBA or any professional leagues for that matter.

Often a big mountain experience is followed by a valley season, but what you do in the valley will determine the kind of success you will ultimately achieve in life.

Are you on a mountaintop right now, or are you trying to survive down in the valley?

BREAK THE PRESS

It's easy to be great when things are going well, isn't it? When all of the stars are aligning in your world and you're enjoying life up on the mountaintop, it's not hard to keep a good attitude. But when you're going through a valley season, it can be very difficult to do so with a winning attitude. Kent Benson did, and it benefited him; it'll benefit us too. Whether you're battling a serious illness or dealing with financial problems or navigating a challenging relationship, it can feel like you're all alone in the valley. But hang in there! Keep moving! You may have to encourage yourself moment by moment but do whatever it takes to get going back up the next mountain.

SLAM DUNK

When you accomplish something amazing or fulfill a dream you've been chasing, make sure you take time to enjoy that moment. Celebrate! Have a party and surround yourself with people who will celebrate with you. Too often, we breeze past our successes because we're ready to climb that next mountain, but don't rush it. Take a few mountaintop selfies and breathe in that air of success. You deserve it.

What is the last major accomplishment you achieved? Did you take time to celebrate? If not, why not?

_____

_____

_____

_____

_____

_____

_____

_____

_____

_____

_____

_____

_____

_____

_____

_____

_____

_____

_____

_____

_____

NOTE

1. Dawn Mitchell, "Top 12 Honest and Controversial Bob Knight Quotes," *Indianapolis Star*, February 8, 2020, https://www.indystar.com/story/sports/college/indiana/2020/02/08/bobby-knight-quotes-honest-controversial-iu-basketball-legend/1631243001.

WEEK 28 | BE THE FIRST

Del Duduit

Steve Downing was a force on the basketball court for the Indiana University Hoosiers.

He stood 6'8" and weighed 225 pounds. His presence on the hardwood could not go unnoticed. When he attended George Washington High School in Indianapolis with teammate George McGinnis, he helped guide them to a 31-0 season and a state championship in 1969. Then it was off to Indiana, where he played in some memorable games.

Perhaps one of the best performances he turned in was during one particular contest against Big Ten rival Michigan. On that night, he recorded the university's first triple double in history. The center scored a game-high 28 points, pulled down 17 rebounds, and added 10 blocks in the 88–79 win at the IU Fieldhouse.

Later the same year, but in the following season, on December 11, 1971, he poured in 47 points and controlled the boards with 25 rebounds in a big 90–89 double-overtime win against Kentucky. He went on to play for the Boston Celtics in the NBA, where he helped them win a title in 1974. But he will always be on record as the first player in IU history to record the coveted triple double.

What can you do each day to the be the first?

BREAK THE PRESS

You are a happy and satisfied person in life. Maybe you have a wonderful job that you love and are married to your best friend. Or perhaps you're in college and planned out your goals to be successful. Or you might be cruising along in life without any major complaints at all. But still, you have an empty feeling inside. You believe you have more to offer, but you're not sure what to do. You're talented and educated and have a passion for life. What can you do? How can you make a positive difference in the lives of those around you?

SLAM DUNK

There are many ways to have an impact on those around you and in your community. You can start by believing in something greater than yourself. You can make a difference in your surroundings with the simple belief that life does not revolve around you. Make it a point to consider the problems in your local neighborhood and pick one to focus on and try to solve. Demonstrate humility and compassion, and keep in mind that one good act can lead to another. What may seem small to you may be significant to someone else. For example, if you paid for a cup of coffee for a person behind you in the drive-thru, that might just make their day. You have no idea what they may be going through, and one act of kindness could set off a chain reaction.

We can all try to inspire one person each day. Start out by complimenting a coworker or sending out a positive note on social media. This is something I try to do each day, and the responses are encouraging. The next thing you can do is find a cause that is close to your heart and get involved. You can volunteer and support it financially. If you can't find one you can become passionate about, consider beginning a local chapter and working for a cause. At times, you might feel lonely or that you're operating solo, but that's okay. Inspire others to join your team. Civic groups are always looking for people to get involved. Be that person. There are many ways you can make a difference in the world and in your community. Become a Big Brother/Big Sister, or take donuts and coffee into a hospice unit at night for the nurses on shift. Take time to send out a card or a text to someone you haven't seen in a while.

Steve was the first player in Indiana University history to record a triple double. It was an amazing accomplishment, but it did not just happen. The result of that one game was the product of years of practice and dedication. You may never know how your generosity impacts others, but rest assured your efforts will not go unnoticed.

Be the first person each day to make a difference. How can you have an impact?

_____

_____

_____

_____

_____

_____

_____

_____

_____

_____

_____

_____

_____

_____

_____

_____

_____

_____

_____

_____

_____

_____

_____

_____

_____

_____

_____

_____

WEEK 29 | GET THE SHOT YOU NEED

Del Duduit

FEBRUARY 26, 2019: INDIANA 75, WISCONSIN 73

IU's Romeo Langford took advantage of a golden opportunity.

The Hoosiers were in double overtime against number-nineteen Wisconsin and in the midst of a five-game losing skid, as well as a five-game home losing streak. Indiana needed a win in the worst way. The team fought all night long and sent the game into double overtime. But with ten seconds left in the second OT, Langford had a split second to seize on a mistake from a Badger defender. The defense misread an offensive pick and left a lane wide open for Langford to go down with the ball. He did not hesitate. He saw daylight between him and the bucket and made his move.

His game-winning layup capped off a career-high 22-point effort and ended the losing streak to put Indiana back on track. A new and young face was learning to be a leader and to put away any fears or doubt to come through for his team. Two previous times in earlier games, he'd had similar chances to win but failed to connect. This time, he made sure the ball went through the hoop. He did not second-guess himself or look to someone else to lift his team—he accepted the responsibility and delivered the victory. For the Hoosiers, the win was the first home conquest in six weeks. The timing could not have been better.

Do you feel like you're in a slump? Maybe the pressure of life has you in double overtime, and the chances of winning are slipping away.

BREAK THE PRESS

We've all been there. My family and I can relate to busy and eventful schedules. There was one period when I stared at my schedule and thought, "How am I going to get through this?" I had six consecutive weekends where I had to be in different states and three other weeks of extensive travel. I was at my limit, and I extended myself too much, affecting my health. But in the midst of that, I received some happy and fabulous news: my grandson had been born. It might have been a difficult period, but it was also a time of blessing.

SLAM DUNK

Can you relate? Maybe your schedule has been like mine or you feel like you're being pulled in nine different directions. Despite this, there are some things you can do to take advantage of the defensive mishap and drive the lane.

Always know that challenging times will pass. I knew once I got through that busy time, life was going to return to normal. Know your purpose and what motivates you to keep going. For most people, it's family and loved ones. Take a few moments to get away with them and recharge. This might be on the way home from work or on a Sunday drive. Make sure you are around people who care for you, and always keep your passion alive and burning. Langford was surrounded by his team and gained support. His desire to win, even though the team was having a losing streak, fueled his fire.

Life is better when you combine wisdom with perseverance. The determination to succeed is essential. Be kind to yourself and others. Life is not a bed of roses for anyone, and all of us share a balance of good and bad times. Embrace the positive moments and learn from the ones that are unpleasant.

Difficult times make us stronger emotionally and teach us to be brave. Equip and prepare yourself with the mindset that no matter what happens or how tough circumstance become, you can motivate yourself to get through the tough times. Langford saw the opening and darted to the basket.

Always keep your head up during a losing streak. If you don't, you might not see the defense make a mistake.

_____

_____

_____

_____

_____

_____

_____

_____

_____

_____

_____

_____

_____

_____

_____

_____

_____

_____

_____

_____

_____

_____

_____

_____

_____

_____

_____

_____

_____

_____

WEEK 30 | GRACE UNDER PRESSURE

Michelle Medlock Adams

YOU KNOW THAT OLD SAYING "all publicity is good publicity"? Well, I'm not sure that's always the case. Take, for example, the story of Damon Bailey. He started making headlines when he was in junior high because he was enormously talented—and because Coach Bob Knight came to one of his games. Then, author John Feinstein wrote about Damon in his book, *Season on the Brink*, when he quoted Knight as saying, "Damon Bailey is better than any guard we have right now. I don't mean potentially better. I mean better today."[1] Add to that Bailey's stellar high school career, breaking record after record, and leading Bedford North Lawrence High School to a state championship his senior year in front of forty-one thousand people and a national television audience, and Damon Bailey had a lot to live up to when he began playing at IU. He was an easy target for haters, especially in the form of fans of the opposing team.

That was certainly the case when IU traveled to Columbus, Ohio, to face the Buckeyes one Sunday afternoon in February 1991. From the moment Bailey took the floor, the OSU students hurled ugly comments and hateful insults at the freshman from Heltonville, Indiana. Every time he got the ball, they chanted and berated him, but he never let it shake him. Bailey didn't respond with any hand gestures or verbal retaliations. No, he let his performance do the talking and answered them with 32 points and no turnovers. OSU went on to win that day with a shot in the last three seconds of the second overtime, but Bailey won a victory too. He proved that he was worth the hype. And he proved he could keep his cool in the face of adversity.

The late Ernest Hemingway once said "courage is grace under pressure,"[2] and I couldn't agree more. To be able to respond and not react, to be able to perform under pressure and not crumble, to be able to take the high road when everything in you wants to retaliate . . . that takes great courage and a healthy dose of self-discipline. How many of us would have hurled a few comments right back at the OSU fans? I know I would've. (In fact, I did—from my living room.) But Bailey held it together, and so did the rest of the team. With their emotions in check, they played their hearts out through regulation and two overtimes only to suffer a heartbreaking loss. True, the Hoosiers lost the battle that day, but they won the war. They demonstrated they could hold their own against second-ranked OSU, and Bailey proved he was the real deal.

What do you have to prove today? How do you handle pressure? Do you exhibit courage?

BREAK THE PRESS

"Respond, don't react. Take a deep breath. Walk away. Don't be a slave to your emotions." You've probably heard all this advice before, but hearing those words of wisdom and acting in accordance with them are two very different things. It's always easier to lash out, but that rarely produces the desired end result. It's better to hold your tongue and let your actions answer for you—just like Damon Bailey did when the OSU fans taunted him. Bailey didn't have to defend himself or say ugly things in return. His actions and talent—scoring 32 points, making no turnovers, and managing to keep OSU's Jim Jackson scoreless during the two five-minute overtimes—spoke volumes.

SLAM DUNK

Some people struggle with being quick to anger. I've heard some say, "Well, that's just the way I'm wired" while others blame their heritage, a lack of sleep, or even being "hangry." But honestly, those are all just excuses for a deeper problem—no self-control or a lack of self-discipline.

Studies have shown that those who have a higher degree of self-control rarely allow impulses or feelings to dictate their decision-making. Thus, their emotions do not rule their lives, which results in a happier, more successful life. So, how do you develop greater self-discipline? The first step is identifying your weaknesses. Self-awareness is healthy and will be the first step down that road to freedom. Practice having more self-control every chance you get, and reward yourself when you see improvement. If you find that your anger is deeply rooted, it might be time to see a pastor or therapist or simply to talk with a good friend who can be your accountability partner.

Try taking the high road and see how high it will take you!

What are some triggers for you—things that make you lose it? How can you grow in self-control this week?

_____

_____

_____

_____

_____

_____

_____

_____

_____

_____

_____

_____

_____

_____

_____

_____

NOTES

1. Scott Henry, "Indiana Basketball: Ranking the 5 Most Hyped Recruits in Hoosiers History," Bleacher Report, May 19, 2013, https://bleacherreport.com/articles/1644294-indiana -basketball-ranking-the-5-most-hyped-recruits-in-hoosiers-history#:~:text=1.,Damon%20 Bailey&text=On%20page%20232%20of%20.

2. Ernest Hemingway quoted by Dorothy Parker, "The Artist's Reward," *New Yorker* 5, no. 21 (November 30, 1929): 28–31.

WEEK 31 | CONTINUE THROUGH THE STRUGGLES

Del Duduit

TED KITCHEL WAS A HOMEGROWN Indiana boy from Howard County. He grew up in Cass County and loved to play basketball. He learned and developed his skills on a makeshift basketball rim in a toolshed at his home.

In high school, he led the Lewis Cass team to an undefeated 20-0 season and a sectional title in 1978. He blitzed the nets with a 26.2 points-per-game average and tossed in 13 rebounds per game to boot. He graduated as the school's all-time leading scorer.

He chose to play at Indiana, but he was limited to only one game his freshman year due to an injury. The Hoosiers captured the 1979 National Invitational Tournament crown without him, but he was happy for them and supported his team.

His sophomore year, he was able to recover from his injury and was used as a backup in a reserve role. He played a big part in the team's 1981 National Championship by averaging 9.9 points per game. He worked hard and aspired to be a starter one day for Coach Bob Knight. During his junior and senior years, he was a true star of the team.

Ted was a consistent scorer and posted an average of 19.6 points per game as a junior and 17.3 points as a senior. The summer before his senior year, he and teammate Jim Thomas represented the nation when they were named to the USA Men's National Team in the 1982 FIBA World Championship in Colombia. Following graduation, he played professionally overseas. He later retired and returned home to Indiana to work as a color commentator for local and regional television.

He is loved and admired by all Hoosier fans because of his work ethic and his comeback from an injury to play like a champion and help win a national title.

BREAK THE PRESS

Have your dreams been put on hold by unforeseen circumstances? Perhaps you have been overlooked for a professional promotion, or your company is downsizing, and your future and savings are in jeopardy. Ted did not expect to be injured his freshman year, but he didn't give up. He worked hard and fought back to make the starting lineup and contribute to winning the title.

SLAM DUNK

There are no guarantees in life. In fact, you will likely face more adversity than championships in your journey. The key is to learn how to handle the disappointments and still come out a winner. Your attitude frames your triumphs over tragedies in life, and a positive mindset is critical. Letdowns will come, and you must be tough in order to push your way through them. Take responsibility for what happens to you and do not make excuses. If something happens outside of your control, then accept it and move forward. Don't take no for an answer. Seek solutions and let each triumph inch you closer to your overall goal. When you lose a game, don't blame the referee. Look back and count the missed free throws and turnovers you committed. Learn from your mistakes and focus on the hard work it takes to become a champion.

How can you overcome your struggles?

_____

_____

_____

_____

_____

_____

_____

WEEK 32 | GO THE EXTRA MILE

Michelle Medlock Adams

DURING LANDON TURNER'S CAREER AT Indiana University, he started in 43 out of 92 games, scoring 688 points and pulling down 348 rebounds. Then, on July 26, 1981, Landon's life was changed forever when he was involved in a car accident that left him paralyzed from the chest down. Coach Bob Knight, who had been hard on Landon when he'd played for him—because he wanted to get the most out of such a talented player—jumped right in following Landon's accident, raising over $400,000 to help with medical expenses. And Coach Knight's intervention didn't stop there. Knowing that Landon had been heading toward a promising NBA career before the accident, Coach Knight wanted to help him realize his dream. So, right before the NBA draft in 1982, Knight got in touch with Boston Celtics president Red Auerbach and proposed an idea that Auerbach agreed to: on their final pick, the Celtics chose Turner.

Turner later told ESPN how surprised he was. "It was close to my heart when they drafted me,"[1] he shared, noting that Auerbach sent him a couple of championship watches over the years. Though Turner's spinal cord injury left him in a wheelchair, it didn't prevent him from going back to IU to complete his degree and attending team events. He stayed connected to IU and Coach Knight and became a symbol of hope and determination for Hoosier fans far and wide.

In 2012, the night before Turner was to be inducted into the Indiana University Hall of Fame, Coach Knight sent him a very meaningful letter by way of Bob Hammel, Knight's friend and a former *Herald-Times* sports editor. While the letter is too lengthy to print in full, I want to include part of that letter that was shared by the IU superfan Chronic Hoosier on their blog:

> Then came your summertime accident on the way to King's Island. Only through great will and determination did you even survive. Your life was changed forever, and you would never experience what you were going to be as a basketball player—the best in the country. But what you did become, Landon, is the most amazing human being—the greatest example of dealing with and overcoming adversity—that I have ever known. There is no player of all the great, great kids that I have coached that I respect more than you. . . . And you also gave me my most unforgettable and meaningful moment on a basketball court. It was at one of our Senior Days. You had come down to be part of it—I always appreciated that—and you were in your wheelchair on the court behind me when on the spur of the moment I asked all the former IU players in the stands that day to stand. Then I thought of you, looked back, and needled you as always: "Landon, aren't you going to stand up?" You gave me that great big smile and said, "Coach, I am standing, in my heart." That, I'll never forget.[2]

Going the extra mile for a friend is always the right thing to do, though it's rarely convenient or easy. Coach Knight went the extra mile for Landon Turner, and their friendship continues. When things get tough, real friends find a way to help. They do their best to make things better. And if they can't change a difficult situation, they stand with their friend for as long as needed.

Are you that kind of friend?

BREAK THE PRESS

I'm not here to convince you to be a Bob Knight fan. Someone who doesn't admire him as much as I do could write a scathing piece, pointing out all of the controversial things he has said and done over his coaching career, but here's the thing—you have to look at a person's entire life before passing judgment. This applies to more than just Coach

Knight. People are too quick to judge others based on individual happenings, not on their hearts. Don't be too quick to judge your friends, your family, or even strangers. The Scriptures say that love believes the best in others. Let's start walking in love.

SLAM DUNK

Are you a good friend? Are you there for the people in your life who really need you? The gift of friendship is so precious, and it's one that is worth your time investment. Look for ways to be a blessing to your friends and family. Think of ways to make life easier for your loved ones.

What are some ways you can bless your friends and family this week?

_____

_____

_____

_____

_____

_____

_____

_____

_____

_____

_____

_____

_____

_____

_____

_____

NOTES

1. Wendell Maxey, "Landon Turner Remembers Life Before Wheelchair," ESPN.com, June 30, 2010, https://www.espn.com/espn/page2/index/_/id/5357655.

2. Chronic Hoosier, "A Letter from Bob Knight to Landon Turner," *Hoosier Chronicles* (blog), November 3, 2012, http://www.hoosierchronicles.com/2012/11/a-letter-from-bob-knight-to-landon.html.

WEEK 33 | THE SIXTH MAN

Michelle Medlock Adams

WHEN COACH TOM CREAN RECRUITED Will Sheehey for his 2010 IU roster, Sheehey already had offers from Stanford, Northwestern, and George Washington. Later, he would receive offers from Michigan, Arizona State, and Georgia Tech. But Indiana fans are eternally thankful that this Stuart, Florida, native chose to share his talent as part of the Hoosier family.

Even as a freshman, Sheehey brought an excitement and tenacity with him that resonated with IU fans everywhere. In fact, he scored his first points as a Hoosier in the season opener against Florida Gulf Coast, quickly driving the lane for a layup and connecting on a free throw after being fouled. It was like he was saying, "Hello, Hoosier Nation. . . . I'm here to play." And so he was.

He played in thirty-two games that year, starting in seven. His sophomore year, he played in thirty-one games, earning a starting position in the last eleven. During his junior year, Sheehey averaged 9.5 points, 3.7 rebounds, and 1.3 assists per game. Many will remember Sheehey's 9 for 9 from the field performance when Purdue came to Assembly Hall that year. Crazy good! Rightfully so, Sheehey won Big Ten's Sixth Man of the Year Award for his steady and much appreciated contribution to his team.

By his senior year, Sheehey had earned a starting position in every outing (except the one game he missed due to an injury). He averaged 11.4 points and 4 rebounds, shooting 47.2 percent from the floor and leading the team in steals with 28 in all. He scored in double figures in nine of the final ten games, finishing with 1,120 points for his time at IU and securing the thirty-seventh spot in the all-time scoring list at IU. The media also named him an honorable mention All-Big Ten.

According to Sportslingo.com, a sixth man tends to be a player who is "a proven scorer and will be substituted into the game in order to add a scoring spark, or to maintain the scoring ability of the team. In addition, the sixth man is a player who's [*sic*] minutes tend to be in line with those of the starting lineup, playing equal or slightly less minutes than the starters."[1]

Sheehey was an ideal sixth man while at IU, and according to BTN.com's Sean Merriman, Sheehey ranks third in his list of Big Ten Sixth Man of the Year recipients of all time, following only Draymond Green (MSU) and Daequan Cook (OSU).

You see, every time Sheehey came into a game, he brought enthusiasm, drive, determination and spunk—not to mention a whole lot of talent. He was often the shot in the arm his teammates needed to get back on track and win the game. He was that guy.

Are you that guy? Are you known for being someone who exudes energy, enthusiasm, and a special kind of talent that makes everyone around you better?

BREAK THE PRESS

Here's the thing about being the sixth man—you have to wait your turn. Sheehey didn't start in every game his first couple of years, but he often played more minutes and scored more points than the five guys who did. As a sixth man, you have to be okay with that. You have to be able to put your ego aside and focus on what's best for the team. It's not easy to do, but when you do it well, you can become more valuable than the five others who beat you out for a starting position. Are you willing to be that sixth man on your team? At your company?

SLAM DUNK

Pride is a tricky thing. It's a cousin to confidence but not a very desirable relative. It's good to have goals and to set your aim high, but in doing so, you have to keep your desire to succeed in balance with your supporting role. Confidence can drive you while pride can keep you from contributing the minute you're asked to sit the bench. In order to be a great sixth man (or woman), you may have to swallow that pride sometimes, and you may have to wait for your chance to shine, but your time is coming! If you feel you've been overlooked for a starting position, let that feeling drive you to perform even better the next time you are called upon.

Can you be a great sixth man? Or are you too concerned with getting all of the spotlight all of the time?

_____

_____

_____

_____

_____

_____

_____

_____

_____

_____

_____

_____

_____

_____

_____

_____

_____

_____

_____

_____

NOTE

1. "Sixth Man," SportsLingo.com, accessed December 15, 2020, https://www.sportslingo.com/sports-glossary/s/sixth-man/.

WEEK 34 | STEPPING INTO GREATNESS

Michelle Medlock Adams

BEFORE DAN DAKICH BECAME A popular podcaster and successful radio host and sports announcer, he was successful at many other things having to do with basketball—coaching men's basketball at Bowling Green for ten years, acting as director of basketball operations at IU, and later serving as the interim head coach of IU after Kelvin Sampson's exit.

Of course, Hoosier fans most remember Dakich as beloved number 11, the 6'5" guard from Gary, Indiana, who played his guts out for Coach Bob Knight from 1981 to 1985. While donning the candy stripes, he achieved much, such as serving as team captain his junior and senior seasons, helping win a Big Ten title, and making three NCAA tournament appearances, to name a few. But more than any other feat, Dakich is revered by Hoosier fans far and wide for single-handedly stopping Michael Jordan in Indiana's spectacular victory over North Carolina in the 1984 NCAA tournament.

The 1984 Tar Heels were a force to be reckoned with for sure. They had four top-ten NBA draft picks that year, so there were several Tar Heels to contend with, but the most talked about, and for good reason, was Michael Jordan. Coach Knight assigned the task of guarding Jordan to Dakich. Jordan scored four points in the first minute of play, but that would not be a true indication of his performance that game. He missed several open shots and ran into early foul trouble, forcing him to the bench for a bit. Dakich, who was playing with a stomach virus, stayed on Jordan and held one of the greatest players who has ever graced the hardwood to only 9 points on his watch. Then Dakich fouled out late in the game and watched Jordan score 4 more points before the final buzzer, but it wouldn't be enough for a Tar Heel victory. The final score: Indiana 72, North Carolina 68.

After IU won the game, one of the reporters grabbed a few Indiana players to comment on taking down the Tar Heels. The reporter asked Steve Alford about scoring 27 points against such a great team while Dakich listened and tried not to vomit. Dakich later told writer Michael Rosenberg in a 1998 article that he couldn't figure out why CBS Sports had wanted to talk with him at all. He remembered saying, "What do you want with me? All I did was throw up in a bucket while the game was on the line."[1]

Dakich didn't even realize what an amazing feat he had accomplished—single-handedly shutting down Michael Jordan—until the reporter asked, "How did you stop Michael Jordan?"

Without hesitation Dakich answered, "It wasn't that hard."

Of course, few knew just how big of a deal that really was because Jordan had only just begun showing the world his greatness, but Hoosier fans knew Dakich had stepped into a bit of greatness of his own that night. All Dakich knew was that Coach had called on him to guard Jordan, and that was what he had done.

Now, more than three decades later, we're still talking about it, writing about it, and cherishing it. You see, you never know when you'll be called upon to step into greatness. I'm sure Dakich wouldn't have chosen that night, with him battling a stomach virus, but moments of destiny choose you. Your job? Be ready.

BREAK THE PRESS

Have you ever experienced any moments when you could sense something big was about to happen? Defining moments have a way of sneaking up on you and usually come at a time you wouldn't have chosen, yet they present themselves anyway. Those are the moments when you have to act. You have to be ready to seize the day, so to speak. Does it take courage? Sure does! Just ask Dakich. But it's always worth it in the end—again, ask Dakich. I'm sure he'd tell you that was one of the greatest nights of his life, even though he was unaware of its magnitude while it was happening. History has a way of putting things into perspective. What will history say about you?

SLAM DUNK

When you prepare for greatness, you'll be ready for those defining moments. You'll be ready to make history. If Dakich hadn't practiced hard and studied game film and had the determination to play through sickness, he would have missed that moment. Let me ask you this: are you preparing for greatness?

What hindrances in your life are keeping you from stepping into greatness? What can you do to prepare for those moments?

_____

_____

_____

_____

_____

_____

_____

_____

_____

_____

_____

_____

_____

_____

_____

_____

_____

_____

NOTE

1. Michael Rosenberg, "Once Upon a Time, There Was a Man Who Stopped Michael . . . ," *Chicago Tribune*, June 13, 1998, https://www.chicagotribune.com/news/ct-xpm-1998-06 -13-9806130154-story.html.

WEEK 35 | BREAK THE BARRIER

Del Duduit

DECEMBER 4, 1948: THE DEBUT OF BILL GARRETT

The 1947–48 season was a bit dismal. Indiana finished 8-12. But the next year, the Hoosier basketball program not only made a complete turnaround, it also helped shape society and established a new standard.

Bill Garrett was a fantastic basketball player from Shelby, Indiana. But he was African American, and very few teams offered roster spots for Black players back then. But Indiana was different and opted to give Bill a chance to play for the Hoosiers. On December 4, 1948, he became the first African American to play for IU at the Old Fieldhouse. His impact was immediate as a sophomore, and he helped the Hoosiers achieve a 14-8 season—a vast improvement from the previous season.

Bill also became the first African American to play in a Big Ten conference game for IU, on January 8, 1949. He was not the first Black player in the conference to do this; that distinction went to Richard Culbertson, who had played for the University of Iowa in 1946. Big Ten teams did not recruit players of color in the segregated 1940s era. Even though there were many talented Black high school basketball players who lived in the Big Ten conference states, they were not recruited. There was an unwritten agreement in the Big Ten that kept these players off the teams.

In August 1947, civil rights activist Faburn DeFrantz, the executive director of Indianapolis's Senate Avenue Young Men's Christian Association, met with IU president Herman Wells, who had previously said he wanted to make integration at Indiana one of his top priorities. DeFrantz and others lobbied on Garrett's behalf to give him a chance to play basketball at IU. Wells conferred with Coach McCracken, who made the decision to let Garrett try out for the team and agreed to let him play if he qualified. Bill made the squad in the fall of 1947—the same year Jackie Robinson broke the color barrier in baseball.

In his first season on the varsity team, Garrett scored 220 points, the highest total for an individual on the team that season. He played his final collegiate basketball game on March 5, 1951. During his last year at IU, the team's overall record was 19-3, and the Hoosiers were ranked seventh in the country.

In his senior season, Garrett's IU teammates voted him most valuable player. Big Ten coaches and numerous sportswriters also acknowledged his talent, voting him to the All- Big Ten first team. He was named All-American, and coaches picked him as a write-in for the college all-star team after his name was left off the ballot.

BREAK THE PRESS

Have you encountered a setback in your life? Maybe you have run into obstacles in your job that keep you from being promoted. Or perhaps you struggle with a personal relationship and are discouraged or afraid it might come to an end. No matter what barriers you face in life, there are ways to overcome them and be victorious.

SLAM DUNK

You know you have talent and are a good person. You have the education and the desire and drive. All you need is the opportunity to play and show your ability. The last words you ever want to hear are the ones that apply: Be patient. Your day will come. In the meantime, be action-oriented and don't lose sight of your dream. Trust your ability and view each opportunity as a platform to grow. Lean on friends and never doubt yourself. Lastly, don't be afraid to fail. Obstacles placed in your way are opportunities for you to learn and prepare for that day when you start on the varsity team for the first time.

How can you prepare to overcome your barriers?

_____

_____

_____

_____

_____

_____

_____

_____

_____

_____

_____

_____

_____

_____

_____

_____

_____

_____

_____

_____

_____

_____

_____

_____

_____

_____

_____

_____

WEEK 36 | BE A TRUE FRIEND

Del Duduit

A. J. Guyton made an immediate impact on the Hoosiers when he arrived in Bloomington in 1996. The Peoria, Illinois, native was a four-year starter for Coach Bob Knight and never missed a game at Indiana. By the time he graduated, he had become the school's all-time leading scorer in three-pointers with 283 and placed fourth in all-time scoring with 2,100.

And there's more. He also finished ranked eighth in all-time Indiana in assists with 403 and tenth in steals with 128. He was definitely a balanced player. During his freshman year, he became only the second player in school history to earn 400 points, collect 100 steals, and dish out 100 assists. He made the All-Big Ten team his sophomore season and was named a preseason All-American both his junior and senior years.

A. J. was outstanding his senior year. He averaged 19.7 points per game and could not be stopped by his defenders. He was named the Big Ten Co-MVP and was selected as a First-Team All-American.

Toward the end of A. J.'s time as a Hoosier, a former teammate publicly accused Bob Knight of choking him in practice a few years before. A. J. and some other players on the team stepped up and called for a press conference to defend their leader. He wanted to give his point of view as a four-year starter who played for the Indiana legend. He spoke with passion and determination and made sure people knew the Bob Knight he played under. He also suggested that bringing forth allegations during a season showed disrespect for the players and the program. He described his tenure at Indiana as the best four years of his life and added he would go back and do it over again if he could.

When his coach came under fire, A. J. stood up and made sure his voice was heard. He did not sit back and shake his head. He acted and made people aware he had Coach Knight's back.

On June 10, 2014, A. J. was informed that he would be inducted into the Indiana Basketball Hall of Fame. He is remembered as a great player who accomplished a great deal on the court. But what he did off the court and from behind a microphone depicted his character.

BREAK THE PRESS

How would you act if someone attacked the reputation of someone you admire? What if a person insulted your spouse or made fun of your child? The first reaction would be to launch a counterattack or maybe even become physical with the accuser. A desire for vengeance and retaliation is normal. But the last thing you want to do is become violent or engage in a verbal altercation. When it comes down to it, there is no way to defend a lie. This has happened to a lot of people, including me. I have had lies told on me, and my wife's integrity has been compromised by people who did not know the truth. It happens. But there are positive ways to handle situations like this. A. J. came to the rescue of his coach because he felt Knight's reputation was under fire. He spoke of his experience only.

SLAM DUNK

You have a few options to pick from when someone attacks someone you love. One thing you can do is sit back and do nothing. Calling out a liar isn't always the best strategy. Consider the consequences and ask yourself if it really matters. You can also choose to deflect the situation with humor. Some lies are too large to ignore, but small ones can earn a playful comment. The final option you can entertain is to call out the person who is making the accusations. Make sure you have the evidence you need to make a strong defense and prove your theory. When you have your friends' and family's backs, people will respect you. You have an obligation to defend the honor and integrity of those you love. Take the high road.

WEEK 37 | LIVE UP TO YOUR POTENTIAL

Del Duduit

STEVE ALFORD: 1983–1987

Elvis Presley said it's difficult to live up to an image. Famous people are still human, and it's hard to live up to their fans' expectations.

When Steve Alford put on an Indiana jersey to play for Bob Knight, he quickly earned a good reputation. The shooting guard from Franklin, Indiana, became a fan favorite. His tough-as-nails play combined with his stubborn attitude to win was a magnet for the faithful following.

Steve personified the image of David, who took on and defeated Goliath. His spirit was that of the team players in the blockbuster movie *Hoosiers*. He did not fit the role of the average number-two guard. His stature was 6'2" and 150 pounds. But his heart was that of a giant.

Steve was considered to be slow, and his reactions were a bit off. He knew his weaknesses, and that made him tough. He committed himself to a strong work ethic and spent a year putting on weight and muscle. The 1993 Indiana Mr. Basketball became a legend for his work ethic on and off the court. In his personal workouts, he would select a spot on the court and take a series of ten shots. If he did not connect on 80 percent, he would enact his own punishment of either wind sprints or fingertip push-ups.

During Steve's four years at Indiana, Coach Bob Knight said the guard pulled more out of his ability than anyone he had ever coached. The 1987 Big Ten Most Valuable Player was a two-time First-Team All-American and led the team to an NCAA title in 1987. He was also known as a dead-eye clutch free-throw shooter. Steve swished 535 of 596 attempts from the charity stripe for an incredible .897 percentage. By the end of his college career, he had scored more than 2,400 points and earned a reputation as a hard-nosed player who gave his body to win. This was his image. He gave it his best, and it showed.

Living up to an image is one thing, as Elvis said. But what about your potential? Do you know your weaknesses? Are you aware of what you can do with your talent and ability?

BREAK THE PRESS

Perhaps you find yourself in a situation where you know you can contribute more to life than just working a nine-to-five job. Maybe an unpredictable life circumstance has forced you to assume a role you didn't expect to fulfill.

SLAM DUNK

It is never too late to fulfill your potential. I did not chase my ambition to be a writer until I was fifty, and some people have waited even longer than that to do what they love. Colonel Sanders, who founded Kentucky Fried Chicken, was sixty-two before he turned his company into a franchise that would later sell for several million dollars. If it happens early in life, that is fantastic. The opportunity might present itself later in life, and that is fine. Just be ready.

In the meantime, there are some things you can do to prepare yourself for success. Steve committed himself to personal workouts after the team practiced. You can do the same. View each day as a new challenge. Demonstrate a positive personality and wear a smile even when you face difficult times. Be proactive and present solutions instead of problems. Make sure you focus on what you can accomplish now and what can wait for another time.

Live each moment to the fullest, and be true to you and your family. Always be open to change, and remember to laugh each day, especially at yourself. Never be afraid to fail, and celebrate your victories with humility. Be a servant and find the silver lining in difficult circumstances.

How will you commit to be the best you can for your team?

_____

_____

_____

_____

_____

_____

_____

_____

_____

_____

_____

_____

_____

_____

_____

_____

_____

_____

_____

_____

_____

_____

_____

_____

_____

_____

_____

_____

_____

_____

_____

_____

WEEK 38 | BE READY TO TAKE THE SHOT

Del Duduit

DECEMBER 5, 2018: INDIANA 71, BUTLER 68

Indiana senior forward Juwan Morgan had a terrific game. His 35 points were mainly why the number-twenty-five ranked Hoosiers were still in the contest. But when the game was on the line, it was a freshman who stepped up to make the big play.

Rob Phinisee received the ball with a couple of seconds left on the clock about thirty-five feet away from the basket, between the top of the key and half court. He had no time to think—only a second to react. The ball was hoisted into the air, and it swished through the net as the buzzer sounded. Indiana pulled off a miraculous 71–68 win over Butler at Bankers Life Fieldhouse in Indianapolis, Indiana. For Phinisee, the game-winning shot came on the same court where he had lost a bid to win a high school state championship as a sophomore. He had been ready for the moment and took the shot to win the game.

This game reminds me of the time my youngest son was a freshman on the varsity baseball team. The squad had struggled all season, but the last game came down to a rivalry match between them and the best team in the county, which would go on to lose in the state semifinals. The opponents put their ace on the mound, a kid who eventually played Division I baseball and was drafted. He threw heat and controlled the placement.

My son was at the plate with the winning run on third base and one out in the bottom of the seventh inning. All he wanted to do was put the ball in play. The count was 1-1, and he was a bit nervous. The pitch came, and he swung and made contact. The ball chopped up the middle and scored the senior on third base. His teammates celebrated and lifted my son into the air, carrying him off the field. A freshman had come through because he was ready.

Phinisee had a similar situation and the same response. He wanted the chance to win and put the ball in the hoop. There was no time to think and no time to look for other options. It was his time, and he took the shot to win the game.

Are you ready to take the chance when it's presented to you? You might get only one opportunity to make the score. Are you prepared?

BREAK THE PRESS

Perhaps you are at work one day when an unexpected opportunity comes your way, requiring you to deliver under pressure. Or you receive a call asking you to volunteer for a charity event at the last moment. Will you deliver?

SLAM DUNK

What will you do when the ball is tossed to you with two seconds left on the clock, or you are up to bat in the last inning with the winning run on third base? Can you hit the shot? Will you put the ball in play? Prepare yourself to come through in the clutch, and don't give up. Get your mind ready to meet challenges each day. On your way to work, think of different scenarios and ways to respond. Make sure you toss in difficult situations as well as fun ones. Practice ways you will respond, and don't be caught off guard.

When Phinisee took the pass, he knew time was running out and launched the game winner. When my son saw the ball coming down the middle, he knew he wouldn't get many opportunities like that, so he took the swing.

Don't let the chance pass you by without going for the win. You might have only one opportunity to take the winning shot. Make the most of it.

How are you prepared to take the final shot?

_____

_____

_____

_____

_____

_____

_____

_____

_____

_____

_____

_____

_____

_____

_____

_____

_____

_____

_____

_____

_____

_____

_____

_____

_____

_____

_____

_____

_____

_____

_____

WEEK 39 | ALWAYS SHOW RESPECT

Del Duduit

QUINN BUCKNER: INDIANA GUARD 1972–76

Life works well when there is a chain of authority. This structure has proven to be the backbone and strength of the military, the nation, the education system, and, above all else, the family.

Quinn Buckner knows this all too well and epitomized respect for his leaders. The Thornridge High School (Illinois) product opted to go to Indiana in 1974 and play for Bob Knight. He was a high school standout athlete in both football and basketball. He had an immediate impact on the roster and ended up being a four-year starter for the team.

During his freshman year, the Hoosiers reached the Final Four but lost to UCLA. Buckner's leadership on the court kept Indiana chugging along and guided the team to two straight undefeated seasons in 1974–75 and 1975–76. They won thirty-seven consecutive Big Ten conference games and captured the NCAA title in 1976.

Buckner was a Third-Team All-American player in 1975 and made two First-Team All-Big Ten squads. But his undaunted play and determination were not his best qualities.

He was a leader because he respected authority and his coach, Bob Knight. He later said he had learned early in life to honor the positions of those in leadership when they are right and when they are wrong. For his actions and attitude, Buckner was a team captain for three years as a Hoosier. He not only respected his coaches but earned their respect as well.

Do you respect authority? Are in you a position of power? How do you handle responsibility?

BREAK THE PRESS

Has your boss ever yelled at you? Can you recall a time when a coach got in your face? Or maybe you are in a management position and are frustrated with members of your team. As a parent, what if your child is defiant? How do you handle these situations?

We all face challenges like these in our families, on a team, or in a boardroom. Often the easiest reactions would be to either get up and walk away or defend yourself and fire back. The hardest thing to do is just sit there and take what you might view as abuse, especially when you know you are right.

SLAM DUNK

There must be respect for authority in the workplace and in the home. As a parent or supervisor, you have to set the example for those you lead. Don't be a dictator. Show discipline but refrain from violence. Enforce the rules and make sure there are consequences for not following them. Never show favoritism, and reward good behavior. If you disagree, at least be open to listening to other viewpoints while you hold to your own personal convictions. Just because you don't see eye to eye with someone doesn't mean you have to show disrespect.

As a parent, show your children appreciation for law enforcement and for those who protect and serve the nation. Positions of authority should be honored no matter who occupies them at the time. This goes for teachers, coaches, and parents. Quinn showed his honor for Coach Knight, and they developed a working relationship that produced many victories for the Hoosiers.

And finally, the same applies to your spouse. You are not the ultimate authority of your home. Your spouse has an equal say. Treat them with respect and honor, and your life together will go much smoother.

When you find ways to work together and honor the system of authority, great things can happen. Teamwork and respect go hand in hand and produce winners on and off the court. Rule with love and respect.

_____

_____

_____

_____

_____

_____

_____

_____

_____

_____

_____

_____

_____

_____

_____

_____

_____

_____

_____

_____

_____

_____

_____

_____

_____

_____

_____

_____

_____

_____

_____

_____

WEEK 40 | THE BLOCK HEARD ROUND THE WORLD

Michelle Medlock Adams

MARCH 21, 2002: INDIANA 74, DUKE 73

A check of the box score says the moment never happened. A check of the game footage reveals what took place.

As the Hoosiers fought back against Duke, down by one, they needed to stop Duke's offense. A spirited comeback meant little if the Blue Devils never relinquished the lead. The Blue Devils fed the ball to Carlos Boozer. The 6'9", 280-pound center dominated when he was within five feet of the basket. At the time, he was thought to be unstoppable. He corralled the pass. As he turned, the expectation was another Duke score.

Many times, a player steps aside, avoiding the embarrassment of the impending dunk. Rather than risk a foul, the player may concede a score in some situations. But A. J. Moye reacted without worrying about what could happen. His size and height meant he faced a mismatch. As Boozer turned to dunk it, Indiana's 6'3" guard outjumped Duke's center. Moye blocked Boozer in such a way the play was ruled a jump ball. Indiana fans erupted as Moye made the play no one thought possible. He refused to give an inch. He refused to back down and concede the basket. Instead of stepping aside, he jumped up and catapulted his team forward, shocking the college basketball world.

Moye's moment lives on in the hearts of IU fans everywhere. Amazingly, if you look at Moye's stat line in a box score for that game, it says he had 14 points, 3 rebounds, 2 steals, and 0 blocks. Luckily, Moye had quit reading box scores long before that day. A book by Bill Russell had inspired a middle-school-aged Moye to focus on the wins and losses, not the individual performance. He may not have received credit in the box score, but the game film doesn't lie. The block heard round the world helped the Hoosiers dethrone the defending champions.

Do you need to get credit for what you do, or are you able to look beyond your individual contribution to see the bigger picture?

BREAK THE PRESS

Those who saw the block knew it happened. The official statistics don't give credit to Moye, but such is life. Do you live for the statistics of your life? Is everything based upon receiving credit for what you do? Sometimes, what you do will go unnoticed by others. But let me tell you something—even if it's not acknowledged, what you do makes a difference. Your boss forgetting to credit you for finishing a project well does not erase the fact that the project was a success. Your spouse doesn't utter a word of thanks when you cook supper and clean the dishes after a long day of work? No matter. You still did something worthwhile. Your efforts are not in vain. Instead of focusing on whether your efforts were acknowledged, value your job well done. Feel good about your good work.

SLAM DUNK

Keep focused on the long term. Credit is temporarily given, but the impact of what you do can create ripples for generations. Your extra effort is not in vain. Do it because it needs to be done. Realize what this moment can lead to in the future. Even if no one else notices, you will have the satisfaction of knowing that you did it, and that you did it well. Make the effort for what it will accomplish, not for the glory it may or may not bring. Just focus on what needs to be done, not on the recognition for doing it.

Do you struggle with not feeling appreciated? How can forgetting about getting credit be a positive in your life?

_____

_____

_____

WEEK 41 | COME THROUGH WHEN IT COUNTS

Del Duduit

FEBRUARY 19, 1989: INDIANA 76, MICHIGAN 75

He was a pure shooter.

Jay Edwards had high expectations when he came to Indiana. He had played basketball at Marion, Indiana, and his teammate Lyndon Johnson had guided the Giants to three straight state titles. The team's colors were purple, so the phrase "purple reign" was appropriate for the school. The duo even shared the honor of being named Mr. Basketball in the Hoosier state and together committed to play at Indiana.

Jay was a dead-eye shooter and earned the nickname "Silk" because of his smooth jumper. During his sophomore year, his last before he entered the NBA draft, he averaged 20 points per game and established a record (later broken) of hitting at least one three-point shot in twenty consecutive games. The same season, he led the Hoosiers to the Big Ten title and was an All-American player. But he will best be remembered by the Indiana faithful for his clutch shooting.

On February 19, 1989, the Hoosiers trailed Michigan by 2 points with only seconds to play. Edwards received the pass at the top of the key and let it fly. Coach Bob Knight, who rarely demonstrated excitement, watched the ball snap the bottom of the net as time expired. The buzzer sounded, and Indiana won the conference matchup 76–75, preserving the team's home win streak at fifteen games. Knight ran onto the floor and jumped up and down with enthusiasm.

Edwards had also made a game-winning shot the week before when Indiana had knocked off Purdue 64–62. Although he played only two years at Indiana before opting to turn professional, he established himself as a clutch player. He came through when his team needed him the most. Today, Edwards still holds the NCAA freshman single-game season record for a three-point field goal shooting percentage of 53.6 percent.

The excitement of the moment is thrilling. I remember when my oldest son hit a baseline jumper as time ran out to win the game. Then I recall when my youngest connected on a game-winning single to beat the best team in the state his freshman year of baseball. But these moments didn't just happen. They were the results of years of practice and dedication. They were able to come through in the clutch because they had mastered the fundamentals of being a good player.

Are you willing to put in the time as a person of integrity to come through for your family?

BREAK THE PRESS

You don't have to hit a buzzer-beater or strike out the side with the bases loaded to be a meaningful member of your team. Your family and friends need a steady leader who is always there, not just a player who wins the games in the end.

SLAM DUNK

Good leaders are there for you in both good times and bad. They are present for the little things in life as well as the major events. Going fishing with your son or daughter means just as much as helping out with homework and being there to kiss a forehead in sad moments. In order to be a steady player, take responsibility for your actions. Live up to your promises and deliver on time. Step up to challenges and own up to your mistakes. Honor your word and be an inspirational example of what a person should be.

List three ways you can come through when your family needs you the most.

_____

_____

_____

WEEK 42 | HELPING OTHERS SUCCEED

Michelle Medlock Adams

YOGI FERRELL

Most people dream of being a hero and excelling as the leading scorer, able to shoot from anywhere on the court and sink it. They want the glory but forget the importance of including others in the story.

Yogi Ferrell proved to be a great all-around player, but helping others succeed cemented his place in Indiana Basketball history. The product of Park Tudor high school gave a glimpse of what was to come when he led in assists in the McDonald's All-American game and tied the record for number of assists in the state championship game.

Yogi's streak of over sixty games with at least one successful three-pointer speaks to his shooting talent. He appeared in more games than any other Hoosier—a stat that reveals his consistency and his drive. But what best tells Yogi's story is his place atop the all-time assists chart. Though he could shoot the lights out, he looked for his teammates and helped them succeed. Team success meant more to him than his own personal accomplishments.

In January 2016, Ferrell led the Hoosiers to an epic beatdown of the Fighting Illini. He scored sixteen, including five three-pointers, but it was his nine assists that stood out the most. A no-look pass set the record. Ferrell dished to Max Bielfeldt for the layup and, with that pass, took sole possession as Indiana's assist king. Yogi had helped his teammates succeed more than anyone else in the history of Indiana Basketball. He saw where they could make a shot, and he put the ball in their hands.

Following the game, Coach Tom Crean pointed to the accomplishment and the character of his senior. Crean said, "They [his teammates] want Yogi to succeed because they know Yogi is going to find them."[1] He set up others so the team could share in the glory. He put others in a position to win so the team could be successful.

Do you see how an unselfish life leads to a lasting legacy?

BREAK THE PRESS

Alluring as it may be to hoard the spotlight, a lasting legacy is left by those who sacrifice. Helping others succeed never diminishes your success. If anything, it enhances your success and builds on it. Is it best to stand alone or to help others reach the podium alongside you? Though there are voices today that push you to think only of yourself, you can ignore them. Be the person who helps a coworker with a big project, even though it wasn't assigned to you. Be the person who volunteers to deliver meals to the shut-ins in your community and *doesn't* post about what you're doing on social media. Make a difference without making a big deal about it. I promise you, that kind of selflessness will get noticed.

SLAM DUNK

Helping others is never a waste of time. The giving spirit is the mark of someone who understands that life is bigger than just one person. Those who sacrifice of themselves leave a heart imprint on the lives of others, on their companies, their families, and their communities. Selflessness gives others a sense of purpose and value. When you help others, you share in the story of their lives. When you give, you touch far more lives. So, like Yogi, look for opportunities to set someone else up for success. Notice their needs and use your talents. Make time to be part of making an impact.

What are some ways you can help others in your life succeed today?

_____

_____

_____

_____

_____

_____

_____

_____

_____

_____

_____

_____

_____

_____

_____

_____

_____

_____

_____

_____

_____

_____

_____

_____

_____

_____

_____

NOTE

1. "No. 25 Indiana Routs Illinois 103-69 on Ferrell's Big Night," WSBT.com, January 20, 2016, https://wsbt.com/sports/content/no-25-indiana-routs-illinois-103-69-on-ferrells-big-night.

WEEK 43 | ASSOCIATE WITH LIKE-MINDED PEOPLE

Del Duduit

MARCH 11, 1961: INDIANA 82, MICHIGAN 67

For Walt Bellamy, the choice was easy to attend and play basketball at Indiana University.

He did not base his decision on location. IU and Bloomington, Indiana, were 780 miles away from his home in New Bern, North Carolina. But during the summer of his junior year of high school, he met some boys from Indiana and played hoops with them. They got along well and developed a genuine camaraderie. The relationships he built with these players were instrumental in his selection of colleges. It was easy. He became a Hoosier.

The choice appeared to be the right one as Walt not only fit in with the chemistry, he emerged as a leader. When he graduated from Indiana, he did so with the record for the most rebounds in the school's history. He played in seventy games and averaged 15.5 boards per outing for 1,087. But that is not all he did. Walt was an offensive threat too and averaged 20.6 points per game, connecting on over 50 percent of his shots. In his final season as a Hoosier, he averaged an incredible 17.8 rebounds per game, which remains a school high mark. He also holds records at IU for the most rebounds in one season with 649 and the most double-doubles with 59.

Walt went out in style during his final game at Indiana. He blazed away and set school and conference records with 33 rebounds and 28 points in an 82–67 win over Michigan. He was the first player in Indiana to be chosen as the number-one player in the NBA draft and was later named the league's Rookie of the Year. He was an All-American in 1961 and First-Team All-American in 1960. And to think, his decision to play for Indiana was based on friendships he made during high school.

Have you ever influenced someone's selection just with your attitude? Does your outlook on life attract others to be around you?

BREAK THE PRESS

Your actions and how others perceive you are important in everyday life. Suppose your boss wants you to show a new client or employee around the office. What will their first impressions of you be? Will you welcome them, or will you chase them off with a negative attitude? It's easy to get in a rut and complain about life's circumstances. There is no perfect job, and everything has its bad points. But if you are not careful, you can fall into the trap of being negative and demonstrate a less-than-ideal personality.

SLAM DUNK

What choice would Walt have made if the players from Indiana had not shown him friendship? He may have opted for another school where he might not have enjoyed the success he had in Bloomington. Always strive to give a warm welcome to newcomers on your team. Introduce yourself in a polite and professional manner, use appropriate language, and offer to help new people adjust. Take them out for coffee or lunch and good conversation. A new environment can be intimidating, whether starting a job, moving into a new neighborhood, or joining a church. When you are friendly and positive, you will put those around you at ease and make them more comfortable. Pull down the rebound and put it back up for the score to be a positive influence on your prospective teammates.

_____

_____

_____

_____

WEEK 44 | YOU'RE BETTER THAN YOU THINK

Michelle Medlock Adams

CALBERT CHEANEY

As Calbert Cheaney scanned the roster, he wondered if he would be able to make an impact.

Sharing his thoughts later in an interview, Cheaney spoke of how he was intimidated by the guys and wondered how he would fit in on the team. Even Coach Bobby Knight later shared his concerns about recruiting the small forward from Evansville. After all, an injury during Cheaney's senior year in high school had really impacted his confidence.

When Cheaney decided to attend Indiana, he was a very valuable part of the number-one recruiting class in the nation. He just didn't know it yet. As practice began, Cheaney saw that his observation from afar had been misguided. He competed. He held his own. And, he realized he deserved to be on that legendary team. By the end of his freshman year, he averaged 17 points per game. From there, his legacy grew.

Cheaney ended his career as the leading scorer in Big Ten history. The college basketball world recognized him as an All-American three times. His crowning achievements were leading the Hoosiers to the Final Four in 1992 and being named the National College Player of the Year in 1993.

Cheaney's career is revered by Hoosier fans. A perfect leader on some exceptional teams, Cheaney earned the respect of all who played against him as well as those who watched him play. Cheaney's basketball career continued beyond Indiana as the Washington Bullets selected him sixth overall in the 1993 NBA draft. He played in basketball's highest level from 1993 to 2006. And to think, at one point, he wondered if he had anything to offer. Even in the uncertainty of what lay ahead, he took a step toward a dream. All of Hoosier Nation appreciates that he took that step.

Do you fail to see what you have to offer? Are you afraid of taking a step toward greatness because you feel you have less to give?

BREAK THE PRESS

Self-doubt exists in nearly all of us. Though there are some who have an abundance of confidence, most people doubt their own abilities. Are you feeling insecure in who you are and what you have to offer? Keep at it. Take a chance. You will see that you are more equipped than you thought. Resist the urge to be so hard on yourself, and reject the notion that you need to measure yourself according to what you see in others. Drown out the self-doubt so you can achieve greatness in your life and bless others in the process.

SLAM DUNK

Beating yourself up doesn't move you in the right direction. Visualize yourself as a winner! See yourself accomplishing your dreams! You aren't meant to be on the bench. You are called to superstardom in your life. It begins by believing you can excel. No one else will believe in you if you don't first believe in yourself. When you do, it will matter less who else believes in you. You are better than you think. You can do great things. Envision yourself as a champion and work for the achievements you desire.

How does self-doubt keep you from achieving greatness in your life?

_____

_____

_____

_____

_____

WEEK 45 | WHAT DOES YOUR NICKNAME SAY ABOUT YOU?

Del Duduit

NOVEMBER 12, 2010

The good news arrived. Cody Zeller made the decision to play for the Indiana Hoosiers. The seven-foot-tall center/power forward turned down offers from powerhouse programs such as North Carolina and Butler. In high school, he earned the distinguished Indiana Mr. Basketball in 2011 and was named a McDonald's All-American and the Gatorade Player of the Year. He was the real deal.

Cody did not disappoint during his freshman year at IU. He led the team with 15.6 points per game and added 6.6 rebounds while shooting an eye-opening 62.3 percent from the field and 75.5 percent from the charity stripe. If that wasn't enough, he ranked fourth in the nation in field goal percentage and was tops in the Big Ten conference, which also dubbed him freshman of the year. He made such a positive impression that he was named as a finalist for the Wayman Tisdale Award and nominated for the prestigious John Wooden Award and the Oscar Robertson Trophy.

Cody was a sure bet for the National Basketball Association but opted to return to Bloomington for his sophomore year. He admitted in a statement issued by the athletic department that he was not ready to give up on his college experience at Indiana. In the statement, he referred to the Hoosier fans as the greatest in the nation.

He made the right decision, and the following season he led Indiana to the Big Ten title with 16.8 points per game and 8.3 boards. Again, he racked up numerous awards, which included being named an All-American, first-team All-Conference and First Team Academic All-American. At the end of his sophomore season, he opted to enter the NBA draft.

With all the glamour and hype that came along with Cody, he was nicknamed "The Big Handsome" at Indiana because he was tall and good-looking. He was polite and well-mannered. Coach Tom Crean described him as one of the most mentally focused athletes he had ever recruited.

How do others describe you? When they hear your name, what images appear in their minds? What do they think of you?

BREAK THE PRESS

You may be ready to enter the workforce, or perhaps you are about to begin a family. Or maybe you are up for a job promotion or seeking a new employer. No matter the case, your reputation is vital to your success. I have been told over the years that I should not care what others think about me, but that is wrong. How we are perceived does matter. And it also matters to your family and children. You want to make sure that your nickname describes you in a positive light. If this is not the case, there is still time to put forth a better image.

SLAM DUNK

People around you observe you all the time, both at work and at home. The way you respond to certain situations and how you act under pressure will mean something down the road. Character is important to your family reputation and heritage. If you haven't started, you can begin to build a solid reputation and nickname for yourself and your kids. Volunteer at charity events or become involved in youth sports or even in local community organizations. Your name is important as well as how others identify you. Take action now and be remembered and recognized for doing good things for your team.

What are some ways to establish a positive name for yourself?

_____

_____

_____

_____

_____

_____

_____

_____

_____

_____

_____

_____

_____

_____

_____

_____

_____

_____

_____

_____

_____

_____

_____

_____

_____

_____

_____

_____

_____

_____

_____

_____

_____

_____

_____

_____

_____

WEEK 46 | OWN UP TO YOUR ACTS

Del Duduit

MARCH 10, 2013: INDIANA 72, MICHIGAN 71

Two things happened on this day.

What fans remember the most is Cody Zeller making a go-ahead layup with thirteen seconds left in the game. He then altered a possible game-winning shot by Michigan's Trey Burke at the other end of the court. These two plays within seconds of each other gave Indiana the win over the Wolverines and their first outright Big Ten conference regular season title in more than twenty years. Burke's game-winning attempt was tipped by Jordan Morgan, but it rolled off the rim. The win was huge for Indiana, but the loss affected more than just number-seven ranked Michigan.

The Ohio State Buckeyes, ranked fourteen, and tenth-ranked Michigan State both needed the Hoosiers to lose in order to share the conference crown. But IU was selfish. Indiana was down by five points in the last minute of the game. Michigan had a chance to increase the lead but failed to connect at the free throw line. Glen Robinson III made one of two tosses, and Zeller connected to cut the lead 71–68. Michigan's Tim Hardaway missed the front end of a one-and-one, and the next trip down, Zeller was fouled and put on the line. The Indiana standout swished both of his attempts. Burke then missed a free throw, and Zeller once again answered with the game-winning layup.

The win was enormous for IU, and a celebration ensued. Words were spoken in the heat of the moment. Indiana Coach Tom Crean got caught up in the emotion and said something to Michigan's assistant coach that he later regretted.

When Crean took over at Indiana in 2008, he inherited a program that was weighed down by several NCAA sanctions imposed during the tenure of Coach Kelvin Sampson and his assistant, Jeff Meyer, who was now an assistant at Michigan. After the win, Crean was caught on camera yelling at Meyer and blaming him for wrecking the program. The Indiana coach was restrained by his staff. He realized he was caught up in the excitement of the moment and soon called Meyer to apologize. Crean told reporters that he never should have addressed the issue in the heat of battle after a big game. He said once he said he was sorry, he moved on, and that was the end of the story.

BREAK THE PRESS

Have you ever said something you regret? Of course you have. We all have done that. Words come out with ease, but once they are said, you cannot take them back. Angry exchanges can easily take place in the heat of an argument. You can spout off at your spouse over silly things and hurt them. You can raise your voice in anger at your children and affect their attitudes. You might even scream at your coworkers and create more tension.

SLAM DUNK

Although Crean admitted he should have used better judgment, he opted to ignore his gut and confront the Michigan assistant coach. Once he did this, he knew he was wrong. He put away his pride and called Meyer and expressed his regret. More people need to do this, but pride often gets in the way. Once you apologize for doing something wrong, you allow the healing process to begin. This might be a quick recovery, or it could take time. But the key is to express genuine remorse, admit responsibility, and not shift the blame to someone else. Make amends and take a vow that it will never happen again. Mistakes are common, but taking ownership and action is rare. Crean did it, and that is why he is considered a class act among college coaches.

How can you take responsibility for your words?

_____

_____

_____

_____

_____

_____

_____

_____

_____

_____

_____

_____

_____

_____

_____

_____

_____

_____

_____

_____

_____

_____

_____

_____

_____

_____

_____

_____

_____

_____

WEEK 47 | BE A TRUE LEADER

Del Duduit

1983: WITTMAN NAMED PERSON OF THE YEAR

Randy Wittman is considered one of the best players in Indiana University Basketball history. He was a productive player with a knack for coming through in the clutch. But he is more well-known and admired for his leadership and courage under pressure.

The Indianapolis native roamed the hardwood at IU for Coach Bob Knight from 1979 to 1983. Right off the bat, he was a member of a winning team. During the 1979–80 season, he was a part of the Big Ten conference title squad that advanced to the Sweet 16 in the Big Show. The next season, the Hoosiers won it all when they knocked off North Carolina. Randy played a big role in the title game when he nailed a shot deep from the corner at the buzzer in the first half to give Indiana its first lead of the game. His field goal lifted his team's spirits and gave them momentum at the break. Indiana went on to capture the title 63–50.

The next season, IU was ranked number one and was favored to repeat as champs. Randy was one of three team captains and demonstrated character on the court. But a key injury to Ted Kitchel was devastating to Indiana's hopes of winning it all again. Randy led the team to another Big Ten conference title and into the NCAA tournament, where Indiana lost to Kentucky in the Sweet 16.

For his efforts and his determination, Randy was named Big Ten Player of the Year and was selected an All-American. In 1996, he was named to the Indiana Silver Anniversary Basketball team. After college, he played in the NBA for Atlanta, Sacramento, and Indiana. He later extended his leadership skills as a professional coach, enjoying a successful career in which he is credited with helping to hone the skills of Kevin Garnett in Minnesota.

Randy's leadership in college helped his team reach the ultimate highs, and his skills continued to be noticed at the next level.

BREAK THE PRESS

What circumstances in life are calling you to take positive steps and become a leader? Perhaps your child's Little League team needs a coach, or an organization you admire does not have a local chapter. What can you do? Will you step up and rise to the occasion or sit back and complain?

SLAM DUNK

You have sat on the bench long enough and believe you are ready to get into the game. The time is now for you to step up and take charge. But there are ways to be an effective leader and earn respect from your peers. Never put others down or be dictatorial. Screaming and yelling seldom work to motivate others. Set rules, but don't rule with an iron first. A true leader will understand his or her style of blazing a trail. Encourage others and be creative. When you inspire with calm authority, people take note and listen. Challenge people in your circle to set goals aligned with their abilities, but encourage them to grow and to take risks. Stretch people to their limits, but don't overextend them. Be the example and serve others. Walk the walk and talk the talk. Be prepared to do what you ask from others. Demonstrate passion, and it will spread to those around you. Listen and communicate effectively. Always have a positive attitude and strive to motivate those around you. Learn from your mistakes and laugh often, especially at yourself. Honor your word and show integrity in all you do.

You may never hit a shot at the buzzer to give your team the lead at the half, but you can lift the spirits of those you come into contact with daily. People are looking for a leader—rise up and take on that responsibility.

How can you be an effective leader?

_____

_____

_____

_____

_____

_____

_____

_____

_____

_____

_____

_____

_____

_____

_____

_____

_____

_____

_____

_____

_____

_____

_____

_____

_____

_____

_____

_____

_____

_____

IU COACHES

WEEK 48 | CRITICS—YEP, EVERYBODY'S GOT 'EM

Michelle Medlock Adams

ONE OF COACH BOB KNIGHT'S famous quotes is the poem he recited one Senior Night after the players had given their heartfelt sentiments. It went a little something like this: "When my time on earth is gone, and my activities here are passed, I want they bury me upside down, and my critics can kiss my ass!"[1] Coach Knight had been called out for his bullying behavior and courtside antics in the weeks leading up to the event, and that poem seemed to sum up his feelings best.

Those in attendance laughed and cheered. And, of course, Knight's critics attacked him for stealing the spotlight from his seniors that year. If you're in the public eye for even a hot minute, you're going to have critics. But those who know you best—the ones who are with you day in and day out, who have seen you at your best and your worst and still love you—those are the only voices worth hearing.

Former players have often voiced praise for Coach Knight—not all, but the majority—so that says something. One of Knight's most famous protégés, Duke coach Mike Krzyzewski (who played for Coach Knight at Army), once said, "Outside of my immediate family, no single person has had a greater impact on my life than Coach Knight. . . . Simply put, I love him."[2]

I think sports analyst Dick Vitale said it best when he wrote a special column for ESPN back in 2003. He wrote:

Knight is one of the sharpest minds ever to grace the sidelines. Yes, his tactics may not be what some believe in. Still, when you graduate players, when you win basketball games, and when you do it the right way with integrity and pride and not a hint of an NCAA investigation, that's memorable. . . . I'm not only proud to say he's a colleague, and proud to say I enjoy watching his teams compete, I'm proud to call him a friend. If I ever needed a helping hand, I know I could pick up the phone and he'd give me support. Yes, we have had our battles. But the one thing I know about the man is that he's fiercely loyal, and when he considers you a friend, you can count on him.[3]

Player after player, story after story, would echo Vitale's words.

NBA coach Jim Boylan once said, "He's a lightning rod. You either love him or hate him. But certainly as an opposing coach, you had to be ready for games against his teams, because you were going to get their best."[4]

I fall into that first group.

Listen, there will always be critics, and if you're doing something worth talking about, your critics will find reasons to raise their collective flag of negativity. But don't let their nasty comments and lack of understanding stop you from doing your thing. The critics never stopped Coach Knight; in fact, I think they fueled him. Let's take a page out of Knight's playbook and recite a poem of our own: "Talk all you want. Say what you will. I'll rise to the top. With grace and with skill. And you'll still be talking, 'cause that's all you do. While I'm living my dream with no thought of you."

BREAK THE PRESS

Sure, some criticism is a good thing. If people only praise us all the time, we have no opportunity to grow. But before you receive someone's criticism and take it to heart, know where that comment is coming from. Is it coming from a place of love? Is it coming from someone who wants to see you become all you were created to be? Or is it just from somebody who is jealous, taking a cheap shot?

SLAM DUNK

When someone says something nasty about you, take a moment before you respond. Oftentimes, we react before we've had time to really process what was said and figure out the best way to handle the situation. Sometimes it's best not to respond at all. Critics will always be loud; let your exemplary life be louder.

What are some critical things someone has said about you or to you that have played over and over in your mind? Write them here and then be done with them!

_____

_____

_____

_____

_____

_____

_____

_____

_____

_____

_____

_____

_____

_____

_____

_____

_____

_____

_____

NOTES

1. Robert Pace, "Bob Knight: The General's Top 20 Quotes as a College Basketball Coach," Bleacher Report, March 3, 2012, https://bleacherreport.com/articles/1080495-bob-knight-the-generals-top-20-quotes-as-a-college-basketball-coach.

2. "Coach Mike Krzyzewski Statement on Bobby Knight," Men's Basketball, Duke University, February 4, 2008, https://goduke.com/news/2008/2/4/1382401.aspx.

3. Dick Vitale, "Knight's Positives Outweigh His Mistakes," ESPN.com, February 5, 2003, https://www.espn.com/dickvitale/vcolumn030129knight800.html.

4. Jeff Carlton, "Peers Praise Knight as Top Coach but Admit He Leaves Mixed Legacy," *Plainview Herald*, February 3, 2008, https://www.myplainview.com/news/article/Peers-praise-Knight-as-top-coach-but-admit-he-8444247.php.

WEEK 49 | STRIVE FOR EXCELLENCE AND LIVE WITH INTEGRITY

Del Duduit

WHEN PEOPLE IN INDIANA HEAR the name Everett Dean, many words come to mind. He was a player, a coach, a mentor, a winner, an author, and a servant. But perhaps the following sums it up best: he strived for excellence and lived with integrity.

Everett was born in Indiana and played basketball in college for the Hoosiers. In 1921, he was named a Helms Foundation All-American. From 1924 to 1938, he coached baseball at Indiana University. From there, he went on to coach basketball at Stanford, where he led his team to win an NCAA championship in 1942.

Seven years later, he took over the baseball team at Stanford and guided them to a College World Series title in 1953. He is the only coach to be named to both the Naismith Basketball Hall of Fame and the College Baseball Hall of Fame. In 1965, he was enshrined in the Indiana Basketball Hall of Fame and was the first basketball player at Indiana to be an All-American.

He also wrote two books: *Indiana Basketball* (1933) and *Progressive Basketball* (1942). As a basketball coach, he posted an overall record of 375-217, and in baseball, his record was 296-175-12.

Everett was a winner as a player and coach. But he is regarded in history as a true gentleman who lived his life with integrity.

What will your legacy be?

BREAK THE PRESS

Have you made some mistakes in life? We all have, and I'm sure Everett made some too. But that is not how he is remembered. When athletes or coaches make a mistake, you often hear or read about it. You can re-call the incidents around Tiger Woods' personal life. People remember that. Or maybe when you hear the name Pete Rose, you might think of the ramifications that come with breaking the rules. There are plenty of examples to go around. But when an athlete lives a good life, this should be noted too. Everett apparently lived that type of life.

What about you? Do you want to be remembered as a person with integrity who overcame the odds and proved everyone wrong? Maybe something from your past has you bogged down, or you may have a reputation you don't desire. There are ways to change that.

SLAM DUNK

You might be living the life you desire without any problems or scandals. There are rewards for living a pure and just life. But for those who need to make a clean start, rest assured it's never too late. Realize restoration will not happen overnight; there are steps you need to take in order to repair your reputation and begin a new journey. The first obstacle that might stand in your way is to make restitution to anyone you have wronged. This might be in monetary worth or may include a personal apology. Next, you must value integrity if you wish to be known for it. Always be true to yourself and the convictions you hold dear. Trust your gut instincts instead of seeking validation from others. Make sure you surround yourself with good and honorable people. Hold each other accountable, and always search for ways to improve. Show confidence in yourself. This can be easy when there is nothing to hide from anyone.

Your character is on display each day. What you do when no one is around will tell you a great deal about yourself. Do what's right without regard for consequences, and let your honesty be transparent. You don't have to be arrogant and tell people what you do, but they will notice. Honor your word and be loyal. Accept personal responsibility and be truthful to yourself and your aspirations. Make a positive difference every day.

Can you think of any more ways to live with honor and strive for excellence?

_____

_____

_____

WEEK 50 | BUILT UP, NOT BEAT DOWN

Michelle Medlock Adams

FEBRUARY 11, 1987: INDIANA 77, NORTHWESTERN 75

When Coach Knight made his postgame comments, he sounded like a coach whose team had just lost the game.

Indiana had traveled to Northwestern for a Big Ten showdown. The Hoosiers' win contained a historic moment as Steve Alford tied the Indiana scoring record with a free throw. The accomplishment cemented his place in Hoosier basketball lore. Yet at the conclusion of the game, his coach had a different outlook. Coach Bob Knight saw a shooter on top of a list who hadn't played at the top of his game. The General never shied away from telling the truth.

The Hoosiers had just squeaked out a victory over the Northwestern Wildcats, who were in last place in the conference. And it was Daryl Thomas's career night of 32 points that had secured the second-ranked Hoosiers a W that night.

After the game, Coach Knight blasted everyone on the team but Thomas, his words sharp and unfiltered. He referenced Alford's previous standout performances but offered that his point guard showed no leadership in the game against Northwestern. He summed up the senior's record-tying performance as horrendous.

Alford had a choice to make. He could become bitter at Coach Knight for the coach's viewpoint, or he could grow from the observation. Alford chose to grow. The words pushed the senior to give all he had. Knight's criticism pushed Alford and the team to a national championship.

Years later, when Knight's criticism was replayed to Alford, the team captain still took no offense to the words. He explained to former IU player and sports radio host Dan Dakich that Knight knew how to get the most out of his players. The coach's words, though sharp and painful, came from a heart that wanted his point guard and his team to excel on and off the court.

Can you accept the harsh truth if it is given by someone who cares about you?

BREAK THE PRESS

Some people want only to criticize and tear down. Others, however, are critical because they care. Can you tell the difference? Do you know who in your life truly wants you to succeed? Dismissing constructive criticism is shortsighted. Though a harsh truth stings at the moment, it develops your character over time. Those who want you to excel know when you can do better. They care enough to point it out so you will not sell yourself short or settle for less.

SLAM DUNK

See the heart behind the words. Such a quest can be difficult but being able to see the motive for what was said is imperative. Though we all want praise and adoration, times of reproof and rebuke are equally necessary. If the criticism is legitimate, we are given awareness and an opportunity to grow. To have others care enough that they push you to greatness is a blessing. Take the valid criticisms and use them to become a more complete version of who you are. Guidance comes through painful truths at times, and that guidance might be the only thing that redirects us from a path of self-destruction. Those who truly love us tell us what we *need* to hear, not just what we *want* to hear.

How can you better apply constructive criticism in your life?

_____

_____

_____

_____

_____

WEEK 51 | NOT FIRED, FIRED UP!

Michelle Medlock Adams

COACH TOM CREAN'S DEPARTURE

When news spread of Coach Tom Crean's firing in 2017, some fans were shocked and disappointed. Others, however, had been expecting the change and seemed relieved. No matter where you stood on the issue of his departure, you can't deny that Coach Crean had brought much-needed hope to a battered basketball program when he'd arrived in Bloomington, and for that, I'm forever a Crean fan.

Even after his firing, Crean remained positive. He told *Sports Illustrated* writer Pete Thamel that he still loved IU: "I loved it here. That's not going to change. You can't go loving something every day for nine years and then suddenly hate it. . . . I hope Indiana wins that national championship. And another one. I really do."[1]

Former athletic director Fred Glass offered little explanation regarding Crean's firing, other than saying, "After deliberative thought and evaluation, including multiple meetings with Tom about the future, I have decided to make a change in the leadership of our men's basketball program."[2] And then he offered, "While winning two outright Big Ten titles in five years and being named Big Ten coach of the year, Tom worked tirelessly to develop great young men and successful teams. However, ultimately, we seek more consistent, high levels of success, and we will not shy away from our expectations."

Translation: You didn't add any NCAA championship banners to Assembly Hall. Despite qualifying for four NCAA tournaments and advancing to the Sweet 16 three times, it just wasn't enough to please the university and its supporters and, I suppose, the Hoosier Nation.

Sometimes, as it turns out, no matter how much you give or how hard you work, your best just won't be good enough for the decision makers. But that doesn't mean you stop being your best and giving your all. No, you hold your head up and move on to the next opportunity—just like Coach Crean did. He didn't sit around getting bitter. Instead, he took a job with ESPN as a commentator, stretching himself and embracing the new experience. It wasn't long before the University of Georgia offered him a head coaching position with its men's basketball program; the school held a press conference to announce Crean's hiring on the one-year anniversary of his firing at IU. He continues building that program at the writing of this book.

Life is full of victories and disappointments—sometimes back to back. I mean, who would've thought you could be named Big Ten Coach of the Year in 2016 and be fired from your coaching job the very next year? That's how it played out for Coach Crean. But that wasn't the end of his story; it was just the end of that chapter. If you're facing some disappointments right now or dealing with the loss of a job or the demise of a dream, I get it. We all go through dark times, but here's some good news: morning is coming! Your story is still being written. So follow Crean's example and keep moving forward.

BREAK THE PRESS

Have you experienced a setback in your life recently? Or have you been busting your butt at work and yet your boss never seems pleased? If you feel like your best is never good enough, take a moment to assess your situation. Be honest. Do you need more training or education to go to that next level in your position? Or is it just time to explore other options and search for an employer who appreciates your contribution?

SLAM DUNK

No matter how well-adjusted you might be, getting demoted or fired or passed over for a promotion can be brutal. It can feel like the end of the world . . . but it's not. You will get through this season, and you will be stronger because of it. Dig deep. Put on a brave face. Put on those "big girl britches," as my mama used to say, and step through that next open door. View this season as one of exciting possibilities. Being forced out of that other job (or that past relationship) might just be the best thing that ever happened to you. Now, go forward with your head held high, knowing your best is yet to come.

How can you improve yourself and use this in-between season as a time of preparation?

_____

_____

_____

_____

_____

_____

_____

_____

_____

_____

_____

_____

_____

_____

_____

_____

NOTES

1. Stu Jackson, "Tom Crean Makes First Public Comments Since IU Dismissal," TheHoosier.com, March 21, 2017, https://indiana.rivals.com/news/tom-crean-makes-first-public-comments-since-iu-dismissal.

2. Zach Osterman, "Tom Crean Fired by Indiana after Nine Seasons with School," USA Today, March 16, 2017, https://www.usatoday.com/story/sports/ncaab/bigten/2017/03/16/tom-crean-fired-indiana/99253570/.

WEEK 52 | HOLD ON TO YOUR CHAIR

Del Duduit

FEBRUARY 23, 1985: PURDUE 72, INDIANA 63

The day is remembered every year in Indiana. It's almost as popular as Christmas or one of the five National Championship banners that hang in the rafters in Simon Skjodt Assembly Hall.

Countless articles are written about what happened, and sports shows recall the moment like it happened yesterday. Nearly all Hoosiers know what took place on this day in Indiana Basketball. Many may not know the score of the game, but they have vivid memories of what happened five minutes into the game against Purdue.

Bob Knight's Hoosiers were struggling and had recently lost six of eight games. The Boilermakers got off to a fast start, and Indiana could not catch a break. Within the first five minutes of the game, six fouls were called on Indiana. Coach Knight had seen enough. The losses combined with the frustration of the game all came to a head. He argued his point with the referees and was whistled for a technical foul.

Knight came up out of his chair, much to the approval of the supportive fans who stood behind the floor general. Knight was fiery and unhappy with the way the game was being called. After his technical foul, he let the referees know how he felt. He stormed back and forth, and his frustration mounted. A lone metal chair was within reach and presented itself as an outlet for his anger. As a Purdue player was about to shoot the technical foul, this chair whizzed by the foul line and slid across the hardwood. Knight had tossed the chair from the bench, and it came to a rest on the other side of the court in a row of photographers. He was ejected and suspended for one game and walked into the locker room with the crowd fully behind him.

At the end of the day, Indiana lost the game, but that was a sidebar. To this day, the moment is remembered each year.

I love Bob Knight and the way he coached. He demanded respect and made men out of his players. In my opinion, he's the best college coach I observed in my years as a sportswriter. He knew what it took to be a winner and demanded the same from his athletes.

For Knight, it wasn't about winning as much as it was about performance and attitude. Some did not approve of what he did on that February day, and I fall into that category. But I won't let that incident tarnish his hall of fame record.

Knight let the situation get to the point where his temper got the best of him. Has that ever happened to you? Have the happenings of a routine day pushed you to the edge?

BREAK THE PRESS

You may not have had the pressure of coaching a Division I basketball program like Indiana. But you do run into situations every day that generate frustration. Perhaps you were passed over for a promotion you felt you deserved, or maybe the bills are beginning to pile up and you struggle with how to make the payments. You may be dealing with a personal dilemma or a medical issue that has put you on edge. There are ways to cope with the pressure of life.

SLAM DUNK

The last thing you want to do is something that might embarrass you or your family. Hitting a wall or throwing an item across a floor might seem appealing and might help you blow off steam. It's easy to let your anger out, but that doesn't make it the best option. There are better ways to deal with an annoyance. Walk away for a few moments and gather your thoughts. Knight did not exercise this option. Instead, he acted on impulse.

Another way to handle stressful moments is to journal your thoughts and emotions. You can take a walk or have a discussion with a person you admire and trust. Once you identify your triggers, you will be better equipped to handle situations with a level head. Always approach moments with a smile and a solution. You don't want to receive a technical while your family watches when they depend on you for guidance. There are better ways to handle a situation than throwing something. This will only bring regret.

List three ways you can cope with a situation that could make you angry.

_____

_____

_____

_____

_____

_____

_____

_____

_____

_____

_____

_____

_____

_____

_____

_____

_____

_____

_____

_____

_____

_____

_____

_____

CONCLUSION

Del Duduit

THROUGHOUT THESE PAGES YOU HAVE relived some of the greatest moments in the history of Indiana University Basketball. The program is established and built on tradition and excellence.

You have read about the team's candy-striped warmup pants and how the "William Tell Overture" brings out the undying support of the faithful followers. Their uniforms are simple and without names on the back to promote the complete team effort.

The school has produced many outstanding players over the years and can boast of excellent coaches who have brought out the best for the university. Although winning is what IU Basketball does best, that's not what is the most important factor for the university.

When I think of Indiana Basketball, the word that pops in my mind as easily as a Cody Zeller layup is *tradition*. The Hoosiers are among the most storied programs in the history of college basketball. A 2019 study listed Indiana as the fifth most valuable collegiate basketball program in the country And Indiana has ranked in the top twenty in the nation in men's basketball attendance every season since Assembly Hall opened in 1972.

There is a reason for this. Over the years in other sports, some fans climb on and off a team's band wagon. When a team does not do well, sometimes you see a lot of empty seats. But even when Indiana went through a tough spell—as all teams do—fans still supported the Hoosiers.

Basketball in Indiana is different. It's not so much about winning but more about family. That is what I took away from the research I did for this book. I live in Ohio and cheer for the Buckeyes. But I want to attend a game in Assembly Hall soon. I want to experience the magic I found when I went back through the archives for this project. It has to be there because that's all I read about.

I am convinced there is something special about the Indiana Hoosiers. Maybe that's why I always rooted for them under my breath. If the team I hoped would win it all got knocked out of the tournament, I usually watched and cheered for the Hoosiers because I appreciate what they stand for and how hard they always play on the court.

It's all about teamwork, family, tradition, and winning.

That is Indiana University Basketball.

DEL DUDUIT is a nonfiction author from Lucasville, Ohio. His first book, *Buckeye Believer: 40 Days of Devotions for the Ohio State Faithful*, was a Selah Award finalist at the 2019 Blue Ridge Mountains Christian Writers Conference. His second book, *Dugout Devotions: Inspirational Hits from MLB's Best*, and third book, *First Down Devotions: Inspiration from the NFL's Best*, were both released in 2019.

As a former sportswriter, he has won both Associated Press and Ohio Prep Sports writing awards. His weekly blog appears at delduduit.com, and his articles have been published by Athletes in Action, *Clubhouse Magazine, Sports Spectrum, The Sports Column, One Christian Voice, The Christian View* online magazine, and *Portsmouth Metro Magazine*. His blogs have appeared on *One Christian Voice* and its national affiliates across the country, on ToddStarnes.com (of Fox News), and on *Almost an Author* and *The Write Conversation*.

During the November 2017 Ohio Christian Writers Conference, Del was named Outstanding Author and received first place awards in both Short Non-Fiction and Inspirational. At the 2018 OCWC, he received first place for Short Non-Fiction.

He and his wife, Angie, are the coeditors of Southern Ohio Christian Voice (sohiochristianvoice.com). Follow Del on Twitter: @delduduit.

MICHELLE MEDLOCK ADAMS is an award-winning journalist and best-selling author, earning top honors from the Associated Press, the Society of Professional Journalists, the Hoosier State Press Association, the Selah Awards, the Golden Scrolls, the Maxwell Awards, and the Illumination Awards.

Since graduating with a journalism degree from Indiana University, Michelle has written and published more than one hundred books with close to 4 million books sold. She has also written more than fifteen hundred articles for newspapers, magazines, and websites; acted as a stringer for the Associated Press; written for a worldwide ministry; helped pen a *New York Times* best seller; hosted "Joy in Our Town" for the Trinity Broadcasting Network; blogged twice weekly for *Guideposts* from 2013 to 2015; written a weekly column for a Midwest newspaper; and served as an adjunct professor at Taylor University three different years. Today, she is president of Platinum Literary Services, a premier full-service literary firm; chairman of the board of advisors for Serious Writer, Inc.; an on-line instructor for the Serious Writer Academy; and a much sought-after speaker at writers' conferences and women's retreats all over the United States. When not working on her own assignments, Michelle ghostwrites articles, blog posts, and books for celebrities, politicians, and some of today's most effective and popular ministers.

Michelle is celebrating the recent releases of her books *Dinosaur Devotions* (Tommy Nelson), *What Is America?* (Worthy Kids), *They Call Me Mom* (Kregel), and *Platinum Faith* (Abingdon). She is married to her high school sweetheart, Jeff, and they have two daughters, Abby and Allyson; two sons-in-law; one grandson; and two granddaughters. (And they all love persimmon pudding!) She and Jeff share their home in Southern Indiana with a miniature dachshund, a rescue shepherd/collie mix, and two cats. When not writing or teaching writing, Michelle enjoys hiking the Milwaukee Trail, bass fishing, and cheering on the Indiana University Basketball team and the Chicago Cubbies. To learn more about Michelle, sign up for her newsletter, or read her weekly blog, go to michellemedlockadams.com.

CPSIA information can be obtained
at www.ICGtesting.com
Printed in the USA
JSHW041906210421
13792JS00001B/2